CANADA WIDE
MEDIA LIMITED

*Provided to the delegates of the Health Work &
Wellness™ Conference 2009 with
compliments from:*

*Canada Wide Media Limited, the largest
independently owned publishing company in
Western Canada.*

*Wellness Matters, a quarterly employee
health and wellness newsletter available in
both English and French version,
print or digital format.*

CHOICES FOR HEALTHY LIVING

Wellness

HEALTH
FITNESS
NUTRITION
WELL-BEING **Matters**

health |
WORK & WELLNESS™
CONFERENCE 2009

Taking Care of Business

The Power of Tact

Peter Legge
with
Tashon Ziara

EAGLET PUBLISHING

Eaglet Publishing
Peter Legge Management Co. Ltd.
4th Floor, 4180 Lougheed Highway
Burnaby, British Columbia, V5C 6A7 Canada
Tel. (604) 299-7311 Fax (604) 299-9188

Library and Archives Canada Cataloguing in Publication Data

Legge, Peter, 1942-
    The power of tact / Peter Legge with Tashon Ziara
ISBN 978-0-9781459-2-7

1. Tact. 2. Success. 3. Self-actualization (Psychology)
I. Ziara, Tashon II. Title.
BF637.S8L45357 2007   158.1   C2007-904976-1
Second printing

Jacket design by Catherine Mullaly; cover image Veer;
Typeset by Ina Bowerbank; Edited by Kim Mah;
Printed and bound in Canada by Friesens Corporation

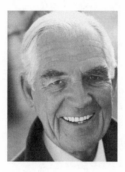

Dedicated to
my father

Bernie Legge
1912 – 1997

Never accept failure or success,
Neither need be permanent.

– Bernie Legge

Other books by the Author

How to Soar With the Eagles
You Can If You Believe You Can
It Begins With A Dream
If Only I'd Said That
If Only I'd Said That, Vol. II
If Only I'd Said That, Vol. III
If Only I'd Said That, Vol. IV
Who Dares Wins
The Runway of Life
Make Your Life a Masterpiece

Booklets

97 Tips on How to Do Business in Tough Times
97 Tips on Customer Service
97 Tips on How to Jumpstart Your Career

CD
The Runway of Life

Acknowledgements

Almost 40 years ago, my wife Kay and I bought a hot dog stand called "Bunny's" at the annual fair in British Columbia, the Pacific National Exhibition. This 17-day fair attracts over a million visitors each year and traditionally signals the end of summer in our province.

That particular summer, it rained almost every day of the fair. And in my first business venture, I ended up losing money. But I learned a valuable lesson.

I quickly realized that it takes a lot of people to make any venture a success. And the better the people, the greater the success you'll enjoy. Writing and publishing books is no exception.

The Power of Tact is my 11th book, and I am proud that each of my previous books has become a Canadian bestseller.

I am just as proud of the team that has come together to produce *The Power of Tact*:

Kim Mah — Our quiet, professional and dedicated editor and proofreader. With the eye of an eagle, she is the best.

Cathy Mullaly — The art director for *BCBusiness* magazine (which was honoured as the B.C./Yukon Magazine of the Year at the 2007 Western Magazine Awards). Her talent for inspired design is evident in this dust jacket.

Ina Bowerbank — Our typographer extraordinaire. Her incredible attention to detail can be seen throughout this volume.

Corinne Smith — Canada Wide Media's Vice President, Production. Her reputation for juggling so many projects all year round, on time and on budget, is a hallmark of her success.

Dale Clarke — My personal assistant. There's always so much happening all at once around her. "No two days are alike," she tells me. Whether it's organizing my business, speaking or public service commitments, she keeps the three-ring circus running smoothly — and fun.

Tashon Ziara — My writer, editor and researcher. Always looking for another life experience to enhance a chapter, she has spent many, many hours with me replicating my speeches and bringing the words to life on the page.

This is the team!

From selling foot-long hot dogs to publishing bestsellers — no one can make it without a team.

And this team is the best. Thank you to each and every one of you.

Peter Legge
Vancouver, B.C.

Table of Contents

Foreword

Introduction 11

Chapter 1: The Essence of Tact
  Choose to have a positive influence on the
  world around you 21

Chapter 2: Keep Your Cool
  Maintaining your composure and confidence
  in tough situations 33

Chapter 3: Exercising Diplomacy
  The key to communicating successfully with
  all types of people 45

Chapter 4: The Art of Persuasion
  Expert techniques for exerting influence on the
  actions and attitudes of others 65

Chapter 5: Opening the Lines of Communication
  Strategies to help reduce misunderstandings
  and encourage positive interaction 77

Chapter 6: Conflict Resolution
  Why listening skills are critical to the problem
  solving process 95

Chapter 7: Negotiation
  How your communication style determines
  what you get 107

Chapter 8: When the Going Gets Tough
  Dealing with difficult people 119

Chapter 9: Rules of Engagement
  Using etiquette to ease awkward situations 135

Chapter 10: The Power of Apology
  Taking your foot out of your mouth when you've
  said or done something you regret 151

Conclusion 161

Introduction

June 2007 marked the tenth anniversary of the death of my father, Bernie Legge.

Bernie was raised in a family with nine children and limited resources. My grandfather was a railway porter for British Rail and my grandmother was a scullery maid. Often, they would have trouble putting food on the table for their large family. When he was growing up, my father lived in Barry, South Wales, which was a great shipping port and he would often spend his free time watching the ships going in and out carrying every kind of cargo imaginable.

When he was 16 years old, seeing very little in the way of prospects for himself in Wales, my father ran away to sea, where the first ship he sailed on was called *Vancouver City*.

Vancouver City was owned by the Smith Shipping Line. It was a 9,000-tonne freighter that transported iron ore. In the many times he circumnavigated the globe, my father came into Vancouver, British Columbia, six or seven times.

He met my mother at a dance at the Hammersmith Palais in London, England (they were both fabulous ballroom dancers). He often told me that after the first time he saw her dance, he knew she was the best of the lot. She was strikingly beautiful and a great dancer. They were such a graceful pair that even well into their seventies, when they would get up on the dance floor, people would clear the way just to watch them.

My parents married in London in 1937 and by the time that I came along, my father was 50 per cent owner of a plastics company that was on Wembley Way in London (within sight of Wembley Stadium, site of the 1948 Summer

Olympics). At that time, the whole country was suffering from the devastation of the Second World War and my parents decided that their future was not to be in England.

They spent many hours discussing where they should go, and in the end, the one place my father loved the most was Canada. So they chose to immigrate to Vancouver. It was decided that my father would travel to Vancouver ahead of us. "I'll go there for a year or so to become established and then I'll send for you and Peter," he told my mother.

Having landed on the East Coast, my father travelled by train from Halifax to British Columbia and got off at the last stop in New Westminster, B.C., where he found his first lodging at the YMCA on Royal Avenue. Eager to find a foothold in his new country, he tried his hand at just about everything, including picking blueberries and working as a short order cook at a café on Kingsway in Vancouver. He did whatever he needed to do to earn money, but try as he might, no permanent opportunities came his way.

Lonely and discouraged, a year after arriving in B.C., my father came to the conclusion that perhaps Canada was not the place for us after all. So he accepted a six-month contract working at a smelter in the northern community of Kitimat in order to earn enough money to go back to England. However, just a few days before he was to leave for Kitimat, he heard about a job at a company called Gilley Brothers, which was located on the waterfront in New Westminster. He applied for the job as an inside sales rep selling concrete and other building supplies. Amazingly, he later reported to my mother, he got the job. So Kitimat never happened and he was able to realize his dream of bringing his family to Canada.

The job at Gilley Brothers was a godsend for my father, but it was by no means easy for him. He often mentioned to me later on, that in his early years at the company he was very much an outsider. At the time, Gilley Brothers was one of the foremost family-owned businesses in New Westminster (it later became Ocean Cement, and then Genstar, which is a well-known B.C. company even today).

Bernie Legge ended up working at Gilley Brothers for 25 years until he turned 65. In those days they had mandatory retirement and so when the day came, they thanked him for his service, threw him a party and wished him well in his retirement.

Thankfully, my father wasn't quite ready to rest on his laurels just yet. When he first retired, I had just purchased *TV Week* magazine, so he decided to come to work with me to negotiate the placement of our magazine racks in retail stores across the Lower Mainland — we thought it would take three or four months, but he ended up staying with the company for 20 years.

Looking back, a great deal has happened in the decade since my father left us. In terms of milestones, the most significant one is that our rival, *TV Guide* magazine, which was formidable competition for several decades, decided in late 2006 to cease publishing the printed version of their guide. As a result, we acquired their Lower Mainland and Vancouver Island subscribers from them, boosting *TV Week*'s circulation by 50 per cent.

Interestingly, we would not have been in a position to take over the *TV Guide* subscribers if not for the fact that my daughter Samantha had taken her MBA at Royal Roads

University in Victoria where her thesis was based on how to rejuvenate *TV Week*. As a result of implementing her plan, today *TV Week* has a 90,000-per-week paid circulation base and I believe that my father would have been so thrilled to know that our little TV listing magazine is enjoying such longevity.

My father was always very kind and tactful with people and I learned a great deal from his example. Today, many of the lessons that he passed on to me remain fresh in my mind and a guiding force in my everyday interactions with others.

Perhaps one of the most important and practical among the lessons that my father imparted to me was the lesson that the best way to get along in life is to exercise the power of tact in all that we say and do. It was a lesson that my father did not preach so much as practice it himself every day. In fact, his enthusiasm for the subject was such that he carried a small booklet entitled *Tact* written by Sir John Lubbock (1834-1913) in his top inside suit pocket every day for as long as I can remember. Someone, perhaps one of his many clients, had given it to him during his time at Gilley Brothers. And the booklet wasn't just for show, either. As I recall, my father often took it out to read over particular passages and he made notes to remind himself of certain aspects of the wisdom contained within its diminutive pages.

"For success in life, tact is more important than talent," wrote Lubbock in the opening paragraph of the book. "But it is not easily acquired by those to whom it does not come naturally. Still, something can be done by considering what others would probably wish."

Consideration of others, this was the cornerstone of Bernie Legge's code of ethics and it is a legacy that he passed on to me, to my three daughters and everyone who benefited from knowing him, including the scores of contestants whom he coached and groomed over the years as emcee of the Miss New Westminster Pageant (part of the Hyack Festival).

Among the many people he touched with his kindness was Leeanne Mueller, who sent the following letter to my family upon his death:

> For Peter, Kay, Samantha, Rebecca and
> Amanda,
>
> I was deeply moved to hear of your recent loss. Bernie's exuberance left its lasting impression on a great many people — as it certainly made one with me. His positive outlook and zest for life has been inspirational! I can still see him answering "Great!" emphasized by a slight swing of his fist, when he was asked "How was your weekend?" or "How is the new play?" He taught me that no one wants to hear negative responses even if things are less than wonderful.
>
> He once shared a book with me titled Tact — something which in the brashness of my twenties was difficult to practise and now, thanks to him, comes much easier as a parent nearing 40. His own diplomacy has been renowned by all whose lives he touched. His head held high, his charming smile, he personi-

*fied the man who knows the secret to a happy
and successful life . . .*

With deepest respect and heartfelt condolences,

*Leeanne Mueller (former circulation director
with TV Week Magazine)*

I've often heard it said that when you know that you're
dying, the last words you say are generally the absolute
truth. Three days before he died, I was sitting with my
father in his private room in the Royal Columbian Hospital
in New Westminster when he told me something that made
me realize my time with him was drawing to a close.

Although Kay and his three granddaughters had spent
every day with him in his last three weeks, this was a moment
when the two of us happened to be alone. As I sat there, he
reached out, caught hold of my hand and very softly said, "I
will miss you the most, but I am so proud of the son, husband, father and community leader that you've become."

In memory of the tenth anniversary of my father's death
and in celebration of his tremendous contribution to my
life and the lives of so many others, I have written this book
to pass along and share with you, how the Power of Tact
can be a force for positive change in the world.

Now before we begin, perhaps you see tact as something old-fashioned or paradoxical to the way the world
seems to operate today, with so many people focused on
building their own success to the exclusion of everything
else, and I agree that it is. That, indeed, is the whole point
of why it is important. We've lost track of how to take care

of each other and it's taking a toll on the younger generations who are witness to every instance of selfish or destructive behaviour.

It's time that we took a refresher course in how to be thoughtful. As Kent M. Keith emphasizes in his "Paradoxical Commandments," people may not thank you (or even notice) when you do the right thing, but whether they do or not, it will make the world a better place, so "do it anyway!"

In case you're not familiar with the Paradoxical Commandments, they were written by Kent Keith in 1968 as part of a booklet for student leaders. Since then, they have been cited time and time again all over the world, in speeches and articles, in sermons and on the Internet. Copies of the commandments have been pinned up in classrooms, stuck to refrigerator doors, given to grandchildren, students and friends. Mother Teresa even had a copy of them up on the wall of her children's home in Calcutta. A few of my favourites include:

> If you do good, people will accuse you
> of selfish ulterior motives.
> *Do good anyway.*

> People really need help but may attack you
> if you do help them.
> *Help people anyway.*

> The good you do today will be forgotten
> tomorrow.
> *Do good anyway.*

As Samuel Johnson once said, "He who waits to do a great deal of good at once will never do anything."

One of my favourite speakers is best-selling author John Maxwell, and a valuable lesson that he often shares is the 30-Second Rule. It goes like this: each time you strike up a conversation with another person, make a point of saying something encouraging to the other person within the first 30 seconds of conversation. The purpose of the rule is to take your focus off yourself and put it where it belongs: on others, by looking for ways to make others feel good about themselves.

Everybody is fighting some kind of battle today; people need to be uplifted, encouraged, appreciated and made to feel that their dreams, hopes and aspirations are achievable. In a word, they need someone to tell them about hope.

Mary Kay Ash once explained that people want to feel worthwhile in life — she told us to imagine that everyone we meet has a sign around their neck that only we can see. It says, "Make me feel important."

As John Maxwell once told an audience:

- The wrong word said at the wrong time discourages me.

- The wrong word said at the right time frustrates me.

- The right word said at the wrong time confuses me.

- The right word said at the right time encourages me.

For me, Sir Winston Churchill stands out as one historical figure who was able to say many of the right words at the right time . . . with a great deal of tact.

This trait is exemplified in the following story:

One evening, a formal dinner was hosted for some important dignitaries and included on the invitation list were Sir Winston Churchill and his wife, Lady Clementine.

Following dinner, each dignitary was asked by the host to answer the question, "Who would you be in history if you could not be who you are?"

As it turned out, the last person to answer the question was Sir Winston Churchill. As he prepared to give his answer, he got up from his chair, reached out to Clementine and took her hand before saying:

"If I couldn't be who I am, then I would want to be Lady Churchill's second husband."

Tact, diplomacy and encouragement in action, Sir Winston knew just what to say and you can too. As Keith's Paradoxical Commandments so wonderfully illustrate and Sir Winston so aptly demonstrates, the Power of Tact is all about taking personal responsibility for the impact that we have on the individual people we come in contact with, on our community and the world as a whole. It is about demonstrating empathy, thoughtfulness and concern for others. As you'll see in the chapters that follow, when put into practice in everyday life, the simple use of tact can be a powerful force for positive change.

Peter Legge
January 2008

CHAPTER ONE

The Essence of Tact

Choose to Have a Positive Influence on the World Around You

The mouth of a wise man is in his heart; the heart of a fool is in his mouth, for what he knoweth or thinketh, he uttereth.

Recently, I was having dinner with a friend of mine, Tony Galasso, who is the president of the Quebecor World Canada printing company. He was visiting Vancouver with his wife and their seven-year-old daughter, Vivianna, and staying at the Pacific Palisades Hotel.

Now, I wasn't aware of this, but when you stay at the

Pacific Palisades and you have a child with you, the hotel staff will bring a pet goldfish to the room to keep the child company during their stay.

It's a great idea and Tony's daughter loved having the fish. However, when Tony leaned over the bowl to take a closer look at his daughter's new pet, he realized that the fish was clearly bloated and dying.

Knowing that the last thing he wanted his daughter to see when they came back from dinner that evening was a dead fish floating in the water, Tony called the front desk and explained the situation to the staff person on duty.

Sympathizing with her customer's concern for his daughter's feelings, rather than suggest that they simply replace the fish, the staff member instructed Tony to tell his daughter that the goldfish was pregnant before they headed out to the restaurant for dinner — and she would take care of the rest.

Take care of it she did. When the family returned from the restaurant, sitting on the table was a fishbowl that looked exactly like the one that had been delivered earlier, except now there were both a big fish and a little fish swimming happily around inside.

The daughter was thrilled.

"Look, daddy," she exclaimed. "You were right, the fish had a baby while we were at dinner — now I have two pets."

My friend Tony was duly impressed and made a point of personally thanking the young woman at the hotel for her thoughtfulness and for providing his family with a happy memory of their visit to Vancouver. He has also, I am sure, shared this story with many friends and colleagues

— as he did with me — and that's the kind of positive publicity that any business would be happy to have.

That's the Power of Tact in action.

But what exactly is tact?

According to Wikipedia, tact is a careful consideration of the feelings and values of another so as to create harmonious relationships with a reduced potential for conflict or offence.

It has also been defined as: a keen sense of what to do or say in order to maintain good relations with others or avoid offence; and, a form of interpersonal diplomacy — characterized by the ability to induce change or communicate potentially hurtful information without offending through the use of consideration, compassion, kindness and reason.

These are some of the words or phrases that come to mind when I think of tact: exercising discretion, sensitivity to the needs of others, compassion, empathy, kindness, consideration, thoughtfulness, selflessness, benevolence, kindheartedness, being humane, gentleness, showing concern, being attentive, unselfish, caring.

Over the years, tact has been defined by many people in different ways. Here are a couple of my favourite descriptions:

> *Tact is the ability to describe others as they see themselves.*
>
> — Abraham Lincoln

> *Tact is the art of making a point without making an enemy.*
>
> — Howard W. Newton

According to Sir John Lubbock, who first published *Tact* (the book that inspired this one) in 1933, exercising tact is about thinking before you act.

"One great need of the world is more sober, profitable thinking," wrote Lubbock in *Tact*. "People go about their business in a headlong way, never pausing to think of results and possible contingencies that will seriously affect the matter. A great mathematician said that if he had but three minutes to work on a problem on which his life depended, he would spend two of them in considering which was the best way to perform it."

For Lubbock, the employment of tact breeds reliability, an attribute that is much desired in those who hold positions of power.

"When a man is wanted for a responsible position, his shrewdness is not considered so important as the quality of his judgment," wrote Lubbock. "Reliability is what is wanted — will he do the right thing in an emergency?"

Many men are liable to overestimate the value of education, brilliance and keenness, which they think at times may be substituted for a level head and sound judgment, said Lubbock. However, he went on to explain that more important to him are the questions: "Can a man stand without being tripped; and if he is thrown, can he land on his feet? Can he be depended upon, under all circumstances, to do the sensible thing? Has he good horse sense? Is he liable to act prematurely? Does he lose his temper or can he control himself? If he can keep a level head under all circumstances, if he cannot be thrown off his balance, and is honest, then he is the man that is wanted."

At the heart of tact is self-control and determination,

attributes that Lubbock believed should be cultivated in all things.

"Whoever determinedly set about a business, has half accomplished it." Lubbock quoted Sir Walter Scott as saying. "Your motto must be, 'Forward Now!' Do instantly whatever is to be done, and take the hours of recreation after business, never before it. When a regiment is under march, the rear is often thrown into confusion because the front does not move steadily and without interruption. It is the same with business. If that which is first in hand is not instantly, steadily and regularly dispatched, other things accumulate behind, till affairs begin to press all at once, and no human brain can stand the confusion. Be, then, in the habit of punctuality and order. Always have an object in view. Let all your things have their place, and let each part of your business have its time."

Lubbock also put a lot of stock in being nice.

"It's the man with the smile who usually wins out in business, as well as in other walks of life for that matter," wrote Lubbock. "Other things being even, the man in business who gets the most patronage is the one who is always pleasant, always civil, always obviously and sincerely glad to see people . . . it really becomes a pleasure for people to spend money with a salesman who gives a little thought and pleasant attention to each customer."

The essence of tact is to make yourself pleasant in the company of others.

"The art of pleasing," Lord Chesterfield once said, "is the art of rising, of distinguishing one's self, of making a figure and fortune in the world."

However you define it, people with tact instinctively

grasp a situation and put others at ease by being able to say or do the right thing at the right moment. They also understand the importance of stepping up to offer assistance and do whatever is necessary in a difficult situation. That is precisely why Auto-Owners Insurance is at the top of my list when it comes to companies who know how to treat customers and business associates.

With 3,000 speaking engagements under my belt, I have spoken to some of the biggest organizations in North America, flown on almost every airline and stayed at virtually every hotel chain on the continent. During that time I have experienced many different levels of customer service and although I don't have any cause to complain about how I am treated for the most part, one experience really stands out as an example of what an organization is willing to do when taking care of the customer (or in this case, a business associate) is truly its number one priority.

In the autumn of 2006, I had entered into a contract for three speaking engagements with a Fortune 500 company headquartered in Lansing, Michigan. Under the terms of the contract, I was to do one presentation a week for three weeks, which meant that I would be spending a lot of time travelling between my home in Vancouver and Lansing. For those of you who are not familiar, Lansing is not the easiest location to fly into — being about 35 minutes by air from Chicago — and there were certainly no direct flights from Vancouver, which meant that I would be flying into O'Hare first and then transferring.

My first trip to Chicago was uneventful; however, when I arrived there was a four-hour rain delay for the connecting flight to Lansing. When I reached my destination, the weather in Lansing was not much better and as I made my way across the tarmac to the terminal, I completely soaked the only pair of shoes I had brought with me.

My host Jeff Harrold, executive vice-president of Auto-Owners Insurance, picked me up at the Lansing airport and took me to the local Sheraton Hotel, which coincidentally, is owned by Auto-Owners Insurance, the company that had contracted me to speak.

Following a glass of wine and a late dinner, the general manager of the hotel, Cindy Bowen, greeted me by name and asked if I needed anything.

I asked her if I could get my shoes shined as they were wet, dirty and didn't look so good.

She said it was too late that night, but she would arrange to have the shoes shined first thing in the morning before my presentation.

As it turned out, there was no shoeshine stand in the hotel, but that didn't keep the manager from making good on her promise. At 7 a.m. the next morning, as I was taking the elevator down to have breakfast, she stepped onto the elevator along with a shoeshine man. She had called him from another hotel just to do my shoes.

Tact and customer service go together.

When it was time for me to return to Vancouver later that day, it was still very cloudy and raining hard and we weren't sure if the scheduled flights from Lansing to Chicago would run. It was absolutely necessary that I get back to Vancouver before 10 o'clock the next day for my scheduled annual medical check-up (an appointment that had taken three months to get).

The last possible connecting flight was leaving Lansing

at 6 p.m. On the drive to the airport, I told Lee Janis III, vice president of sales with Auto-Owners, that I couldn't miss this flight. Unfortunately, when we reached Lansing airport, all of the flights to and from Chicago had once again been rain delayed.

I was sure that I was going to miss my appointment.

Hearing the news that my flight had been delayed, without a moment's hesitation, Lee said, "No problem, I'll drive you. Just let me gas up the car and off we go!"

I was impressed. On the spur of the moment, he put his plans for the day and evening on hold to drive nearly four hours around the lake to O'Hare just for me. Wow! Not to mention the fact that he would have another four-hour drive to get back to Lansing.

Thankfully, the next three weeks of my engagement with Auto-Owners were not as eventful; nevertheless, every time I came back, Joe the shoeshine guy was in the hotel lobby waiting to shine my shoes — and I never had to fly into Chicago again. Instead, Auto-Owners arranged for me to fly into Detroit where they had a limo to pick me up for the 60-minute drive to Lansing.

Auto-Owners remains one of my favourite clients. They always treat me with an enormous amount of tact and great respect.

As with many things in life, when it comes to exercising tact, what you don't say is just as important as what you do. Here is a poem that appeared in Sir John Lubbock's *Tact*.

DON'T SAY IT

If you think that you are better than your
neighbour 'cross the way,
Or that nature has endowed you with a
more perfect form of clay,
Don't say it.

If you know that you have talent and your
neighbour naught but gold,
Or that all his goods are mortgaged if
the truth were only told,
Don't say it.

If you know some dreadful scandal,
such as gossips always court,
And could add a few words to it when
they call for your support,
Don't do it.

Let your life be true and earnest,
court discretion for your friend,
And though often you are tempted a word to
say that would offend,
Don't say it.

TACTICAL MANOEUVRES

- *Tact involves addressing how we live our lives and the effect we have on everything and everyone around us. Everything we do matters — and makes either a positive or a negative impact. Recognizing how your behaviour affects others and holding yourself accountable for your actions is a step in the right direction on the road to developing tact. Even something as simple as giving the right-of-way to another motorist makes a difference. Recall how great you felt when you have done just this and the other driver has graciously acknowledged you, or when someone has given you the right-of-way.*

- *For many of us, much of life is spent in business pursuits; therefore we all have a vested interest in making those interactions as pleasant and agreeable as possible. Don't rush your interactions with others for the sake of getting more done. Take the time to build real connections and that effort will be rewarded in the long run.*

- *Never underestimate the power of three little words to change the world. They are: I thank you.*

- *Think of some other ways that you can have a more positive effect on others, write them down and then practise them.*

CHAPTER TWO

Keep Your Cool

Maintaining Your Composure and Confidence in Tough Situations

A cool head is as necessary as a warm heart. In any negotiations, steadiness and coolness are invaluable and they will often carry you through times of danger and difficulty.

I like Winnipeg, Manitoba: its big, blue prairie sky; friendly, welcoming people; and the positive way the city gets things done.

What's positive in Winnipeg, you ask? Everything from a self-deprecating joke about the city's famous mosquitoes that rise in black clouds each summer from the flatland waterways, to hearing from a fur-covered, frost-encrusted Winnipeg veteran that he's proud to be living in the world's biggest, coldest city. That's not just talking positive, it's a manifestation of raw courage.

On a sparkling spring day when the last of the winter had gone and the sun flashed up at the aircraft from the pools of melted snow below us, I flew into Winnipeg to make a speech.

I was on a ridiculous schedule at the time. Upon landing, I would grab a cab at the airport, head downtown, make the speech, mingle with the delegates at a conference, sleep, head back to the airport and hop on a plane through Toronto to London, England — where I would do the same thing all over again.

Before leaving Winnipeg Airport to head downtown, I went up to the Air Canada counter, gave them my name and schedule and said to the attendant: "I'm staying at the Westin. It's very important that I be in London tomorrow night. If there are any flight changes, could you please let me know?" He assured me he would.

With confidence — and nice feelings about the assignment ahead — I took the cab downtown, made the speech, went to bed, got up the next morning and caught a cab to the airport to catch the flight that would get me to London. It was another lovely morning.

I walked to the counter, slapped down my ticket and passport and said, "Good morning."

The attendant looked down at my ticket, then looked up at me and informed me that the flight had been cancelled.

You know the feeling you get in a situation like that. The blood moves from the top of your forehead, you drop your shoulders, you assume a fighting, protective stance, a kill-anyone stance. It's a reaction that's latent in all of us and it comes with the human territory.

But we *can* control it.

Miraculously, the reasoning side of my brain clicked in at that moment.

"Peter," it said. "Whatever has happened is probably not the fault of this Air Canada attendant, and it will not do you any good at all to blow up, ruin his day and still not get to London."

So I said to the agent, "I wish you had called me at the hotel. I *did* leave a number."

"Yes, sir, I know you did," he said. "But the cancellation came just a short time ago and we didn't have the manpower to inform all of our passengers."

"Well, no problem," I answered. "You can put me on another flight to Toronto and I can still connect to London."

"There are no other flights to Toronto, sir," he informed me.

I took a deep breath to stabilize my heartbeat and the reasoning side of my brain clicked in again.

"Whatever is now happening is not the fault of this Air Canada attendant, Peter," it told me. "And it will not do you any good at all to blow up, ruin his day and still not get to London."

So I turned to the agent and said, "Is there *any* way at all you can help me get to London today?" There was a note in my voice that I rarely hear. It comes from way down deep in the pleading part of our anatomy and that too is part of the evolution of mankind.

"Just a moment, sir," he said and left the counter.

I stood there half fuming and half in a panic, waiting until he returned — *20 minutes later!*

"Mr. Legge," he said, upon his return. "Here's what I've done."

I knew at that moment that he had solved the problem and I leaned on the counter and listened intently as he explained.

"In 20 minutes you will be leaving on a plane for Calgary."

"Yes," I said.

"An hour after you get to Calgary, you will be connecting with an Air Canada flight out of Vancouver, which, despite some head winds over Greenland this afternoon, will get you into London just two hours later than the original flight you were hoping to take through Toronto, O.K.?"

I reached across the counter, grabbed his hand, shook it gratefully, read the name on his lapel and said, "Thank you, John. Thank you!"

He smiled, then quietly and efficiently checked my luggage, made the computer entry and handed me my baggage tags and tickets. I turned to leave, feeling incredibly elated and relieved.

"Mr. Legge," he called. And I turned. "There are passengers who buy first-class tickets and there are others who are first-class passengers no matter how they fly. Thank you for understanding."

I felt terrific!

Of course, the story proves a point. Is it that you can catch more flies with honey than you can with vinegar? Or that a soft answer turns away wrath?

Yes, it's both of those. But it also proves that even in the most aggravating of circumstances, a little diplomacy and tact go a long way in helping you to get what you want or need. It never makes sense to blow up to make your point or to get angry to get what you want.

It wouldn't have worked in Winnipeg and it doesn't work anywhere. You hurt defenceless people by shouting at them, but you win by understanding their point of view and by giving them the respect they deserve in the job they have been assigned to do.

Almost always, people will come up with extra effort when there's understanding. Shouting at agents and clerks and receptionists and those who have the potential to help will get you quickly to the back of the real or imagined line, a million miles from whatever your destination may be.

When you find yourself in a situation where you think you might lose your cool, count to 10, then begin again as a rational human being. It made Winnipeg a better place that day, and it can make your day, wherever it may take you.

For many of us, the values, habits and manners that we developed during our formative years (or those that were instilled within us) are the ones we tend to carry throughout life. Often, they are the habits and manners of our parents and teachers. I remember my childhood school, Tavistock Hall in England's East Sussex, with a considerable amount of affection. In many ways, the years I spent there were a turning point in my life and it was there that I learned many of the values that would stick with me forever.

Perhaps because of this, when Raymond Ward, the principal of Tavistock Hall, wrote to me in the mid-'90s to invite me to the school's 50th reunion, I eagerly responded and bought a ticket for the event. Remarkably, Ray Ward had kept track of 1,600 boys who had passed through the school over the years and I was on the list.

When the time of the reunion arrived, I flew from Vancouver to London, rented a car and headed south down familiar-yet-not-quite-remembered roads, through the scenery of my childhood. When I arrived at my destination, before checking into a local hotel, I stopped in at Tavistock to soak up some of the '90s atmosphere prior to the party.

Following a few cups of tea, Ray presented me with a picture of the "Father's Eleven," the cricket team of parents that included my own dad, when they played together while I was at school back in 1952. It brought back good memories and it was a wonderful gift.

The reunion itself was to be a fundraising affair for the school and as such included a formal dinner and auction. As the auction got underway during the meal, one item, in amongst things such as a trip to Spain or a beach holiday in Cornwall, caught my attention. It was a book called *Be a Man,* written by H. Bucknall back in 1947 as "a word in season to junior boys" who were in his care while he was principal of the Carlisle Preparatory School.

"Bucky," as he was known, went on to become principal of my school and even though the stamp on the inside front cover showed that the book had been due back at the Tavistock School Library on February 6, 1948, it was now up for auction and I dearly wanted it for my own.

The school custodian, acting as auctioneer for the evening, accepted my opening bid of £5 and in short order, opposing bids that moved the price to £10, £15, £20, £25. When I returned with a bid of £150, the custodian simply said: "I think we'll stop there." And the book was mine. A treasure from another age, the wisdom of a man who felt the urge to give young men a solid foundation from which to launch themselves.

I began re-reading *Be a Man* on the long plane ride home and, despite its sometimes strange language (chapter headings such as "Coming Up to the Scratch," "Facing Difficulties" and "Hardening Up") and philosophy, it really was a great read. Going through it, I tried to visualize the period in which it was written. The Second World War had already been tearing at the graduates of Bucky's school for three years at that time. The headings of the book's 10 slim chapters would perhaps have steeled others for conflict.

As I finished reading the book somewhere high over Canada's Northwest Territories, I reflected on how *Be a Man* influenced my thinking when I first read it in 1946. Bucky was writing for an audience of pre-teenagers, but his rules for life are somehow universal. I can read and react to them now in very much the same way as I did when I was an adolescent. I would like to share some of his wisdom with you here:

"The boy who doesn't, now and then, settle down to some serious occupation of his own free will, whether it is a matter of saying his prayers, reading a good book, or writing a careful letter, is neglecting a most important part of his self training," wrote Bucky. "And his whole character will suffer from that neglect. And don't forget that it is by your character that people will know and judge you, like or dislike you, help or hinder you."

In order to grow, he said, muscles must have exercise. It's the same with the development of the mind and character. If you don't become a responsible person, you will never be an individual of the least importance or gain the respect of people whose opinion is worth anything.

"It is the duty of everyone to try to be of use in the world, to try to live honourable, straightforward, unselfish lives to benefit other people," he counselled. "Only in this way can we do what we are here to do — that is, leave the world a little better for our having lived in it."

"Our motives for doing right improve with our conduct," noted Bucky. "It isn't good enough to live nobly because you want people to say you are a noble man . . . live nobly because you love what is noble and hate what is base, and because you wish to do good in the world by force of a noble example, that is good enough. Nothing, in fact, could be better."

Bad habits, Bucky warned, often begin at a young age. "The habits you form during your boyhood are liable to cling to you all your life and you have to be a very strong-minded sort of chap to be able to break yourself of them."

Boys, he said, can roughly be divided into two classes: those who have a code of honour and those who do not.

"By code of honour I don't mean a certain number of rules which they have learnt by heart . . . but certain fairly distinct notions of what is right and wrong, and an ever-growing inclination to stick to the former and avoid the latter . . . One thing a boy must have is a code of honour. He gets it by deciding for himself very definitively what are the things to do and what are the things to avoid doing."

Bucky noted that patterns of dishonesty are deep-rooted:

"We are apt to think that the piece of dishonesty for which a man, especially a man in a good position, is ruined, is the first wrong he ever did . . . As a rule, he has been doing wrong and foolish things for years, and this last thing is only a trifle more wrong and more foolish than lots of other things he has done, and had, besides, the supreme disadvantage of being discovered."

In his inimitable style, Bucky also covered the subject of tact. "Your simple duty is to avoid doing or saying unkind things and to lend a helping and protecting hand when it is plainly needed," he advised. "When you are a man you will have great need of a particular quality which is calculated not only to make your own life smoother and happier but the lives of those around you smoother and happier too. This is the quality of kindliness. The man who has no kindliness in him cannot be a happy man, because he will live in a world made up of people he doesn't like and who don't like him."

"If you wish people to be kind to you, you must be kind to them, and if you wish people to be generous to you, you must be generous to them. The kindness and generosity you show to others will nearly always bring you kindness and generosity in return."

I may not have known it back when I first read Bucky's book in 1946, but I would take many of his lessons with me through life. They would become good guidelines for business, for building a family, for being a good husband and father. They would be the beginnings of speeches that I make today and will continue making tomorrow. And they are the stuff of books like this one.

"It's the man with a smile who usually wins out in business, as well as in other walks of life," J. Clinton Ransom told us in the introduction to Lubbock's essay, *Tact*. "Sometimes it is surely no easy trick to smile, but the trick in business is to do the hard things. Anyone can do the easy things . . ."

He went on to explain that the practice of courtesy is about learning self-control, "for the courteous man must think of others as well as himself," he advised.

"He must keep his temper under trying circumstances and confine himself to proper language when it is easy to abuse and afterward have much regret."

Therefore, Ransom said, always be polite — at all times, to all persons, old or young, educated or uneducated, rich or poor.

"The importance of this cannot be too highly estimated," noted Ransom. "For a man may be of no consequence today. But he may be a person of wealth and influence tomorrow, and will certainly remember how you treated him when he was not so well situated."

There's no question that interacting with others, particularly people who are frustrated or angry, can be stressful. However, it is best not to escalate the situation by raising your own voice and feeding into the anger. It is far more helpful to stay calm, speak in a thoughtful, concerned manner and try to defuse the situation. If you are able to keep your cool, chances are that you'll be able to communicate more effectively and find a positive resolution to the conflict.

TACTICAL MANOEUVRES

- *"Have the courage of your opinions," advised Sir John Lubbock. "You must expect to be laughed at sometimes, and it will do you no harm. There is nothing ridiculous in seeming to be what you really are, but a good deal in affecting to be what you are not. People often distress themselves, get angry and drift into a coolness with others, for some quite imaginary grievance."*

CHAPTER THREE

Exercising Diplomacy

The Key to Communicating Successfully With All Types of People

Be always discreet, keep your counsel. If you do not keep it for yourself, you cannot expect others to keep it for you.

Variety International is one of the most successful and respected charities in the world. Every year, usually in May, about 800 Variety members from around the world meet for five days to celebrate the successes of the past year and to dream about the future — namely, how to continue creating innovative ways to raise money for Variety's special children.

As a global organization, the location of Variety's annual gathering changes from year to year and one of the happy by-products of being involved is the opportunity to visit different cities.

Some years ago, the global convention was held in London, England, and as part of the agenda, a side trip to Paris was offered.

Paris in the springtime! I wouldn't miss it for the world.

With great anticipation, Jeffrey Barnett, a fellow Vancouverite, who along with his twin brother is a principal of the Elephant & Castle group of companies in Canada and a non-stop Variety worker and supporter, set up dinner reservations at Lasserre, one of the finest and most expensive restaurants in Paris.

There would be five of us dining together: Jeffrey and his wife Hildi, George Pitman (another Elephant & Castle principal and Variety stalwart), myself and my wife Kay.

The night of the dinner, it was a fabulous evening. The restaurant had been, and perhaps still was, an old house. We arrived at the dining area on the third floor via elevator and the roof folded back to leave nothing between us, the exciting air of Paris and the stars in the sky above.

The food, like the evening, was magical. We were treated to a seemingly endless array of courses with classic sauces, delicate accompaniments and wines to match every mouthful. It was, in a word, unforgettable.

When the time came for dessert and the presentation of a menu with the restaurant's classic offerings, printed in English at the very bottom of the menu in tiny script were the chilling words: "We do not accept any credit cards whatsoever."

We couldn't believe our eyes. A meal of gargantuan proportion almost ended and not one of us at the table had any more than a few francs in our pockets. We had simply assumed that they would be willing to accept good old North American plastic.

In a panic, we asked to see the manager to explain our predicament, quite prepared to remain as Paris *plongeurs* for the rest of our lives.

The manager came and listened politely to our story, and then, quite unruffled, asked for a business card, which I immediately presented.

"No problem, monsieur," he said. "At the conclusion of your meal, we will simply invoice you and expect payment in 30 days."

We whooped for joy and dived into the dessert.

Wow! What tact and what trust.

Here was a man who had never seen us before and would not likely see us again, who was quite prepared to assume the risk of payment from a distant country for one of the largest restaurant bills I have ever seen. It was a supremely civilized thing to do and it left us all in awe of the unpredictability of the human race and in praise of the proprietor of the restaurant.

Would the same thing happen in Canada? "Perhaps," we said, but surely not many would risk such a gesture.

We subsequently learned that in 10 years the Lasserre had only been *stung* on one occasion. They offered credit in every sense of the word, but more than anything, they offered the trust they believed would be honoured by guests of the Lasserre, and they were right.

We had a superb lesson in the art of fine dining that

evening in Paris, but even more significantly, we experienced first-hand the genuine meaning of tact and trust.

We live in a world where, unfortunately, it doesn't seem to make sense to put trust to the test. We lock things up, tie them down, ask for payment in advance and require three pieces of identification before accepting that someone is who they say they are.

But what if we started taking tiny steps to treat each other with more respect, to offer our trust in small ways and use tact as our guiding principle in our interactions with others . . . what effect do you think that would have on the world that we live in?

EVERYDAY DIPLOMACY

"Manners are like the shadows of virtues," Sir John Lubbock quoted Sydney Smith in his book *Tact*. "They are the momentary display of those qualities which our fellow creatures love and respect." Manners are a small but significant way of showing those people we come into contact with that we recognize the importance of their needs and wishes in addition to our own.

"Please" and "thank you" are the cornerstones of common courtesy, yet amazingly, many people no longer find it necessary to acknowledge the helpfulness of others — particularly strangers — with these two little phrases. Myself, I am not sure how to account for this change in behaviour. Is it that we have forgotten our manners, or do we think that they no longer matter?

Think about your own behaviour. How often do you

thank others for holding the door open for you, serving you in the grocery or convenience store, handling your complaint about a product or service, or for giving you the right-of-way on the road? When was the last time you wrote a thank-you card as a spontaneous expression of gratitude or used the word "please" when requesting a small courtesy from your spouse, child or colleague?

It's such a small thing, and yet when we do remember our manners, we are often immediately rewarded for our good behaviour with a smile or other friendly gesture. No matter where you go or what you do, you cannot underestimate the positive power of treating everyone you meet with kindness and respect. In fact, whether you speak more than one language or not, you can get along almost anywhere in the world with the simple words for "please" and "thank you."

Here are some questions from my book *Make Your Life a Masterpiece* that will help you to check how well you use your manners or, as I like to call it, your Courtesy Quotient:

- Do you return phone calls and emails in a timely manner?

- Do you regularly express gratitude to those around you, especially when someone has done something nice for you?

- Are you available to others without making them feel as if they're imposing?

- Do you make sure never to keep people waiting more than a few minutes to meet with you?

- Have you trained your staff to respond with courtesy and politeness in all situations?

- Do you regularly ask others for input, and genuinely consider what they have offered?

- Do you notice when people are approaching a building at the same time as you and hold the door open for them?

- Are you generous with compliments and express them when others have done a good job?

- Do you always say please and thank you at restaurants, when you shop and when someone has helped you in some way?

- Do you allow the person with one grocery item to go ahead of you at the check-out?

- Do you allow other vehicles to move into the lane in front of you without honking your horn at them?

- Do you pay your bills on time, or let your creditors know if you cannot?

- Are you cautious about how you speak about others so as not to start rumours or spread gossip?

- Do you make sure never to put down your competitors or speak ill of them?

- Do your customers know that you value them, from your words and your deeds?

- Do you make every effort to curb your tongue when you feel like flying off the handle?

While all of these niceties may seem like small things — it really is the small gestures that we make towards others that leave a lasting impression. If you're not sure how you measure up, do a courtesy check for yourself and make the appropriate adjustments.

Everyday diplomacy is about employing both manners and personal restraint — or tact — in our day-to-day dealings with others.

Although some people may equate being tactful with lying or being dishonest, this is not the case. As a general rule, honesty is always the best policy. However, the truth is not always pretty, and sometimes, blunt honesty can be hurtful; therefore tact is necessary. Tact, though truthful, is never insulting or rude. The art of tact involves phrasing things to avoid hurt feelings and provide constructive criticism.

For example, when your friend invites you to visit their new home — which you think is old and dilapidated — and then asks you, "Do you like my new house?" Do you respond with, "No, it's falling apart, why didn't you buy something newer?" or, "It needs a lot of work, but I know with your handyman skills you'll have it fixed up in no time and the neighbourhood is really great." Or perhaps a colleague whose sense of humour sets your nerves on end asks if you would like to go see a comedy performance with them. Do you respond by saying, "I don't think I'd like it, your sense of humour bothers me," or "I don't really feel like it, but thank you for the invitation."

In each of these situations, there is the potential for hurt feelings or anger. But by emphasizing the positive, you can provide tactfully honest answers that do not offend anyone.

> *If you want others to be happy, practise compassion.*
> *If you want to be happy, practise compassion.*
> — The Dalai Lama

One of the tenets of everyday diplomacy is taking the time to think before you speak. As the saying goes, "It is better to be thought a fool than to open your mouth and remove all doubt." Therefore, a good rule of thumb is, when in doubt, hold your tongue and keep your counsel. Here is an example of what can happen when you don't:

For about 25 years, I have had my hair cut in downtown Vancouver at an excellent salon called Kanai Hairstyling, named after the owner. My personal hair stylist is a young woman named Christine. On my 60th birthday, I was sitting in the chair enjoying a chat with Christine as she performed her usual magic.

As it was a slow day, Kanai himself wandered over and

joined in the conversation. Wanting to acknowledge my milestone, Christine turned to Kanai and said, "You know, it's Peter's birthday today."

Kanai smiled and wished me a happy birthday and then asked me how old I was.

"I'm 60 years old today," I replied.

He looked at me closely and said without hesitation, "My, my, that's amazing, I thought you were 65!"

I'm sure that we can all empathize with Mr. Kanai, having stuck one or both of our own feet in our mouth from time to time. The best that we can do in a situation like this is to apologize profusely or perhaps eat some humble pie (more about that at the end of Chapter 10) and ask for forgiveness. Errors in judgement can often have very public consequences that seriously affect the reputation of the individual or organization involved. If we don't own up to our mistakes, we risk doing long-term damage to the relationship, whether the injured party was a customer, friend, spouse or business associate.

One way to reduce the possibility of misunderstandings is to practice the three C's of communication — be clear, be concise and be courteous. If people can't understand what you're saying, you're not communicating. Therefore, speak clearly and try not to use slang or jargon. After all, your point is to be understood, not to prove that you are hip or cool. The same goes for showing off what you know.

"Never try to show your own superiority," said Sir John Lubbock. "Few things annoy people more than being made to feel small."

It is also true that nobody likes to be treated like a number. Thoughtful comments, conversation or observations can help set a positive mood for your interaction with others. By the same token, all people deserve to be treated with the same degree of respect and diplomacy. You just never know whom you might be speaking with or what potential the interaction might have had, had you simply kept an open mind.

The following story told by John N. Wheeler in *Tact* illustrates the point:

> *A man of my acquaintance once made an early morning call to see a railroad president whom he knew to be temporarily making his headquarters at his New York offices.*
>
> *There was no one at the reception desk when he entered, but in response to his rapping on the desk, a shirt-sleeved man minus collar and tie, apparently a janitor, appeared from an inner office.*
>
> *"Is Mr. Blank in?" the salesman asked.*
>
> *"What do you want?" inquired the other.*
>
> *"I'll tell Mr. Blank that when I see him," the salesman replied.*
>
> *"Go ahead," drawled the man in shirt-sleeves. "I happen to be Mr. Blank."*
>
> *The salesman tried to go ahead, but he couldn't seem to get up steam. And thereafter he was never flippant to anyone in the reception room of any company.*

*Avoid shame, but do not seek glory, nothing is
so expensive as glory.*

— Sydney Smith

Being diplomatic often requires us to let go of our preju-
dices, but that is sometimes easier said than done. Although
few people in today's world would admit that they don't
have an open mind (and of course, everyone has a different definition of what an open mind entails), when it comes
to religion, politics, morals and rules of behaviour, many
of us are pretty set in our ways. Therefore, when somebody
starts presenting what sounds like an opposing view, the
vast majority of us simply switch off our ears and wait for
a chance to use our mouths.

"How could they hold such a preposterous viewpoint?"
we ask ourselves. "Surely, I need to set them straight."

We're all so sure that we're right, that we become more
and more unwilling to even consider the opinions of others. This is a shame, because it seems unlikely that the
world would be a better place if everyone held the same
point of view. But overcoming ingrained attitudes in order
to open up to others is difficult. It's so much easier to stub-
bornly insist that we're right and anyone who disagrees
with us must be wrong, evil, dimwitted or grossly misin-
formed.

What to do?

A good start is to make a conscious effort to suspend
judgement and take a moment instead to ask yourself,
"What would it take to convince me that this person's idea
has some credibility?"

By doing this you will open yourself up to at least consider other points of view, which in turn will leave the door open to explore how those ideas might have some merit. Say, for example, you're a strong believer in self-determination and therefore believe that social programs simply encourage lazy people to live off the backs of legitimate taxpayers. What would it take to convince you that some people need a hand up to get back on their feet? Or, say you think military force is the only way to deal with rogue states. What might convince you that there are other options? Really listening and responding thoughtfully to the ideas of others is a great way to build goodwill and trust in any relationship.

> *At times our own light goes out and is rekindled by a spark from another person. Each of us has cause to think with deep gratitude of those who have lighted the flame within us.*
>
> — Albert Schweitzer

Everything you do counts. Never underestimate the power of a few well-chosen words or a kindly gesture to make someone's day a little better. Following is a case in point:

In 1991 the Sales and Marketing Executives of Vancouver presented me with their Marketing Executive of the Year Award. It was the first award that I had ever received and about 350 guests would be attending a gala awards dinner at the Four Seasons Hotel in Vancouver. One of the speakers that evening was a long-time mentor of mine, Ray Addington, who a few years ago was recognized by his home country of England with the Order of the British Empire.

Little did I know that in addition to the award, Ray had a special gift for me when I stepped up on stage. As I shook his hand, he presented me with a framed letter with the following text:

> *Dear Mr. Legge,*
>
> *My warm congratulations on being chosen Sales and Marketing Executive of the Year by your colleagues. This is indeed a most prestigious award and I am delighted that it is being presented to someone who is not only born in Britain, but who continues to be a great friend of my country.*
> *With all good wishes.*
>
> *Yours sincerely,*
>
> *The Right Honourable Margaret Thatcher, O.M.; F.R.S.; M.P.*

I can hardly describe what a thrill it was to receive this letter and how encouraged I was to continue on my path to building the company that would one day become the largest independent publisher in Western Canada.

Emile de Girardin once said, "The power of words is

immense. A well-chosen word has often sufficed to stop a fly-ing army to change defeat into victory and to save an empire."

Noted *New York Times* best-selling author John C. Maxwell has remarked that "when a word of encourage-ment is written down for another person, it is often per-ceived to be more genuine than when it is spoken."

Great leaders develop the habit of writing tactful notes of encouragement. Since I received the letter from Margaret Thatcher in 1991, this one gesture has caused me to try to do the same for as many people as I can.

So often, it is the small things we do that leave the most powerful impression; remembering a special occasion, ask-ing after someone's sick relative, holding the door open or helping someone into their coat. Ruy Paes-Braga, who is vice president and general manager of the Four Seasons Hotel in Vancouver, personally delivers a handwritten note and a box of chocolates to any employee of the hotel who is celebrating a birthday. Imagine how such a gesture must feel to an entry-level employee who might think that the upper-level management don't even know their name, never mind their birthdate.

Of course, being kind or helpful doesn't mean that you need to be pushy. Being too helpful, to the point of being intrusive, can be just as negative as not being helpful enough. Have respect for the boundaries of those around you; if someone declines your offer of help, don't push it.

When you do offer assistance and it is accepted, make sure that you follow through promptly.

"Preserve your integrity — it is more precious than diamonds or rubies," advised Sir John Lubbock. "Let your pledged word ever be sacred. Never promise to do a thing without trying your best to perform it with the most rigid promptness." And if you simply cannot deliver as promised, follow up with an explanation and an alternative plan.

> *Never intrude where you are not wanted, there is plenty of room elsewhere.*
> — Sir John Lubbock

TACTICAL MANOEUVRES

"The discreet man finds out the talents of those he converses with and knows how to apply them to proper uses," noted Sir John Lubbock. "Accordingly, if we look into the communities and divisions of men, we may observe that it is the discreet man, not the witty nor the learned, nor the brave who guides the conversation and gives measure to the society."

- *Look for opportunities to let others shine and encourage them to use their talents to the best purpose. They will appreciate your confidence in them and others will recognize your skill for spotting the right talent for the situation.*

- *Be sensitive to the feelings of others. Most of the problems we encounter with relationships are emotional in nature and empathy is an important tool that we can use to defuse tension and build understanding. Being sensi-*

tive to the needs and feelings of the people around you can greatly improve your dealings with them. Recognizing when you're stepping on someone's toes, or when a colleague is "not in the mood" for a joke will keep you from getting into sticky situations that are difficult to get out of.

- *Keep your sense of humour with you at all times; you never know when you may need it. Laughter is a great way to break the ice in many situations, and it also goes a long way towards smoothing over uncomfortable moments. The ability to laugh at yourself or to see the humour in the little snafus that we all must deal with shows people that you don't take yourself too seriously. Of course, the joke should never be at someone else's expense — that's just mean.*

- *Open, Sesame! No one enjoys being around a shallow, narrow-minded person, so try to keep an open mind with regard to the viewpoints of others. While others may not say things that you'll always agree with, learning to at least be receptive enough not to be immediately offended by something can go a long way towards diplomacy. Keeping an open mind is a great way to actually turn a potentially troublesome argument into a more productive — and perhaps even fun — debate. Also, give new people that you meet the benefit of the doubt and most likely they will extend the same courtesy to you.*

- *Don't touch that dial. Unless it is an emergency, carrying on a conversation on your cell phone when you are out with someone is a sign of disrespect. If you must answer the phone, keep your conversation brief and let the caller know that you are otherwise engaged. The same holds true when you are being served by someone in a store or restaurant. You wouldn't want to wait for service while they talked on the phone and they deserve the same courtesy.*

- *Was it something I said? "Some people seem to have a knack of saying the wrong thing, or alluding to any subject which revives sad memories or rouses differences of opinion," said Sir John Lubbock. "Avoid unkind and irritating language." Use your intuition to tune in to the effect that your words and behaviour have on others. If you have any doubt at all, ask for feedback or (if you're too embarrassed to ask) simply "tone it down" and see if that has a positive effect.*

- *Follow through on your interactions. Send thank-you notes and include your business card. Communicate your appreciation for being provided the opportunity to serve your customers and make sure they have your contact information should they need further assistance. This small gesture goes a long way toward cementing your relationship with that person. Here are some other situations where a thank-you card is appropriate:*

  - *When you receive a referral for your business*

  - *When you receive a gift*

- *When you receive an honour or recognition*

- *Set a good example. The most effective means of communicating the kind of behaviour you expect from your colleagues, employees, friends, neighbours, your partner or your children is to model that behaviour yourself. If you are rude, dismissive or sarcastic with others, how can you expect anything better in return?*

- *Show respect for everyone you meet. Some people operate under the misguided notion that respect is something that must be earned. This is a wrongheaded notion that can actually cause a lot of relationship problems. Respect should be given freely to others, no matter their point of view or social/economic position, and only retracted if they purposefully do something that you believe to be unethical.*

- *"Nothing is more valuable to a man in business than the name of always doing as he agrees, and that to the moment," wrote Sir John Lubbock. "Remember that punctuality is the mother of confidence." Always be punctual. Everyone is busy. If appointments and meetings are a part of your life, respect other's time by always being either a little bit early or right on time. It demonstrates professionalism, respect and a commitment to keeping your promises. Everyone likes to deal with a person who delivers. This applies to activities with your children as well.*

- *"Many people talk, not because they have anything to*

say, but for the mere love of talking," Sir John also noted. "Talking should be an exercise of the brain, rather than the tongue. Talkativeness, the love of talking for talking's sake, is almost fatal to success. Men are plainly hurried on in the heat of their talk to say quite different things from what they first intended and which they afterwards wish unsaid." Make a point to listen more than you talk and take the time to think through your ideas and opinions before you open your mouth to share them.

- *Be a fire hydrant, not a flamethrower. For most of us, it's all too easy to take sides in an argument or fan the flames of disagreement. But whether it's a discussion about which hockey team deserves to win the Stanley Cup or what to do with violent repeat offenders, if you overdo it, you're asking for trouble. Learn to fix arguments and soothe hurt feelings instead of saying things that will only add fuel to the flames.*

- *There's no "I" in we or us. Getting along with others is all about give and take. While there's nothing wrong with wanting to be successful, happy and loved, just remember that other people want the same things you do. Consider how much easier and more enjoyable life can be when you work together with others to help one other achieve mutually compatible goals.*

CHAPTER FOUR

The Art of Persuasion

Expert Techniques for Exerting Influence on the Actions and Attitudes of Others

Tact often succeeds where force fails.

"We flatter ourselves by claiming to be rational and intellectual beings, but it would be a great mistake to suppose that men are always guided by reason. We are strange inconsistent creatures and we act quite as often, perhaps oftener, from prejudice or passion. The result is that you are more likely to carry men with you by enlisting their feelings, than by convincing their reason," wrote Sir John Lubbock in *Tact*. "This applies, moreover, to companies of men even more than to individuals."

I agree with Sir John. In more than 30 years as emcee for the Variety Children's Telethon, I have seen people moved to great acts of generosity in response to the children we have featured onstage. Here is the story of one such occasion.

This past February, a young boy named Connor had his 10th birthday party on the same Saturday as the Variety Telethon. Prior to his party, rather than have everyone bring a gift, Connor asked all of his friends to bring money instead to help the kids on the Variety Telethon. After the party, he convinced his mom to bring him to the Global TV studios in Burnaby. Connor and his mom arrived at the studio where the show was in progress, with no badge, credentials or appointment, but somehow this little boy and his mom managed to talk their way in until they were standing right outside the door to the main studio where the telethon was airing live. Here they were held back by security, who questioned the pair to find out how they had gotten so far without authorized identification.

Connor told them the story about his birthday party.

Whether it was fate or simply a case of one determined little boy knowing the importance of being in the right place at the right time, as Connor and his mom were standing outside the door, Debbie Scott, who is in charge of all of the finances during the telethon, came out of the main studio and ran into Connor and his mom. After hearing their story, Debbie jumped on the situation and immediately said, "Get Peter, this little boy needs to be on the show."

As I finished a live presentation from another Variety supporter, I was summoned to listen to Connor's story. Immediately afterward, I went to Keri Nelson and Floyd Lansing, the producers of the telethon, and said, "We need to get this little guy on the show before he collapses with nervousness."

Within two or three minutes, they had cleared a space in our schedule for me to interview Connor. I then went back out to see Connor and his mom and said, "Let's go — you're on in 60 seconds."

Suddenly realizing what he had gotten himself into, Connor burst into tears and hid in his mother's skirt, and try as we might, we couldn't get him to move towards the stage.

Running out of ideas, I thought, "Let's get RCMP officer Bob Underhill out here in his full red serge to escort Connor onto the set." Officer Underhill, who stands six-feet-10 in his stocking feet, and in full regalia probably looks to be about ten feet tall, only made matters worse. Connor was scared to death.

Finally, Global news anchor Jill Krop approached Connor and hand in hand, Jill, Connor and Officer Underhill approached the stage while I did a quick introduction. However, when I started to talk to Connor, he still wouldn't say a word, he was so nervous. In a last attempt, I told him just to look at me and tell me what he'd done. As he told the story of his birthday party and his request to his guests, he announced that he had raised $60 for Variety.

The audience cheered and Connor beamed.

Following the surprise segment on Connor, to get back

on schedule the cameras had to return to Global TV's Tony Parsons, who anchors the six o'clock news. Clearly impressed with Connor, Tony said on the air, "Did you see that?"

For those who don't know, Tony's evening newscast on Global TV has the largest TV audience outside of New York, so there were a lot of people watching.

"If Connor can raise $60," Tony challenged the viewers, "what can you do?"

At that point, the phones went absolutely crazy and it was truly a magic moment for the telethon.

Just as charities like Variety are constantly coming up with ways to inspire people to support the good work that they do, so too are business leaders always looking for innovative ways to motivate their employees — the people who collectively do much to make things happen. My friend Joe Segal, who is president of Kingswood Capital Corporation, an organization that, among other things, once owned Mr. Jax Fashions — is a master of motivation. To keep the company on top of the latest trends, Joe required his buyers to travel frequently from their Vancouver base to Toronto and Montreal on week-long buying trips.

Making regular trips to source out the latest styles may sound like a dream job to some, but believe me, as someone who has logged more than his share of travel miles, going on the road and living in hotels, eating in restaurants, having to rely on cabs for transportation and being constantly "on" in an unfamiliar environment, business travel loses its appeal very quickly.

So how did Joe keep his buyers motivated and willing to brave those week-long buying trips? He always sent them off in economy class when they were fresh and ready for the tough road ahead. However, when the deals were done and it was time to head for home, Joe's people always flew first class. It is a carrot that rewards performance — believe me, it works. And boy, do those stretch-out seats and all that service and attention ever feel good!

Of course, some people think that the only way to exert influence over others is by exercising their authority. In my experience, this is rarely advisable.

"The practice of showing authority merely for authority's sake always hurts rather than helps," said J. Clinton Ransom in the introduction to *Tact*. "Executives will be more valuable — they will more easily bring out the best that is in their men — if taught that every subordinate should be a follower, and a loyal follower."

Ransom shared the following story of how one young man's life was changed by one simple, thoughtful gesture:

> *Many years ago there was the head of a well-known firm who liked to tell of his first day with the house. He started as a lad of 16, and on the first day he was set to work sewing buttons on sample cards. The day was hot and sultry. The work of pushing the needle through the stiff cards had hurt his fingers. He was to receive $3 a week and by noon he had planned exactly what he was going to do about the half-dollar he was to earn for the first day's work. He wasn't coming back for it. He was through with that job.*
>
> But then something happened.

During the afternoon one of the members of the firm came to him and said; "You are sewing those buttons on very nicely, but you are not doing it in the best way and you are hurting your fingers. Let me show you how to do it."

The result was that instead of quitting his job, the young man went home and, flushed with pleasure, told his mother how a member of the firm had complimented him and then had shown him a better way to do his work. His enthusiasm to learn responded to this first sign of encouragement and in later years he became one of the strongest forces in the development of a great business.

"How costly to that business would have been the loss of that man!" concluded Ransom.

Better to win people over using the powers of persuasion. Robert Cialdini, Ph.D., who is a professor of psychology at Arizona State University, has developed what he calls the "Principles of Persuasion," which explain the most common means used to influence the behaviour of others. They are:

Reciprocation. People naturally feel obligated to give back to those who have given to them. If you help someone or provide something they need, they will be more open to persuasion and more willing to offer you something in return.

Scarcity. People want more of what they think is scarce.

If you've got exclusive information, people will value it more highly because it's new and fresh.

Authority. People often feel unable to make a decision based on their own information or experience; however, they want to know that they are making decisions based on the best advice. That is why they look to legitimate experts to guide them. Being able to share your expertise is a good way to influence the decisions of others.

Commitment and Consistency. By aligning your request with someone's values, you have a better chance of their accepting your ideas. It is also important to get commitments in writing. People are much more likely to live up to what they agree to in writing.

Consensus: The truth is that most people are followers. Therefore, when they are unsure what to do, they look to what others in similar situations are doing. This is the reason that testimonials remain an important part of marketing.

Liking. It's human nature to like people who like us. It's also human nature to seek out the approval of those who like us. That is why we prefer to say yes, rather than no, when those who clearly like us make a request.

In an essay titled, *Courting Success*, S.M. Kennedy noted that the greatest game in the world is success and that every player is playing his cards to win.

"Success is made up of many attributes and no one element in itself can assure it," wrote Kennedy. "The annals of successful men clearly demonstrate that all such men knew the value of cooperation — could cooperate themselves and always picked assistants who understood the meaning of the word.

"The lives of successful men illuminate the pathway for those who seek the guiding light of experience," continued Kennedy. "All successful men have not reached the goal through the same attributes or by the same means. But all signs point to the quickening power of courtesy and politeness. The influence of a kind act never ends."

To end this chapter, I want to share a story about an elderly lady whom I met during a recent vacation. I think it proves the point that if you really want something in life, you have to speak up and ask for it.

Sitting on the deck of the Seabourn Legend in Italy's Portofino Harbour on the last night of a remarkable cruise through the Mediterranean, I was waiting for my wife Kay to join me on deck for the final night's barbecue. It was a perfectly glorious evening with not a cloud in the sky and it was still at least another two-and-a-half hours before the sun would set.

There I sat with a glass a wine in hand looking at La Cervara, a 13th-century monastery that had been purchased by a billionaire from Milan. He had spent the past three years renovating this exquisite building and it was a marvel to behold. Not a few hours before, we had been sitting in the courtyard of that very monastery, sipping champagne and listening to a string quartet play the classics. Recalling the perfection of the afternoon, the phrase "died and gone to heaven" leapt to mind.

Coming back to the present moment, I struck up a conversation with an elderly woman at the next table. Her name was Sybil Clumpus and she too was enjoying the warm air and the glorious view along with her adult children. They were from the north of England, she informed me and when I asked where the husbands were, she simply said, "We're travelling alone."

Keeping the conversation going, I asked her what her husband did and she replied that her husband, whose name was Sid, had passed away five years ago.

I asked her if she still missed him and I think she wiped away a tear that indicated that she did.

"How did you meet him?" I asked.

"I first met him when I was 12 years old and we became friends, nothing more," she said. "However, when we were both in our early twenties I met a young American man and we became engaged. Less than two months before the wedding, I went to Sid and asked him, 'If I sent you an invitation to my wedding, would you attend?'"

"No," he responded, "You're not going to marry him; you are going to marry me."

"But the wedding is in six weeks," Sybil replied.

"It doesn't make any difference," he told her, "This marriage [meaning Sid and Sybil's] is made in heaven."

"But I don't even love you," Sybil protested.

"But you will!" was Sid's only response.

Sybil never married the American and was instead happily married to Sid for 39 years. Together, they owned and operated a men's clothing store.

Three days before Sid died, he said to Sybil, "When I'm gone, many of the couples we know will likely invite you to join them for lunches and dinners. Remember this . . . remember this, if you want to go a second time, always pay your own way. Because they won't take you for dinner a second or third time if they have to always pay for you."

"That's good advice," I said to Sybil as I thanked her for the conversation and headed off to the barbecue with the love of my life — my beautiful wife Kay. As we strolled along, I couldn't help but smile, wondering just what it was that Sid had done to persuade Sybil to call off her wedding to the American and marry him instead. Considering how I met and married Kay (that story is detailed in my book *The Runway of Life*), I have a feeling that Sid and I would have gotten along famously.

TACTICAL MANOEUVRES

- *If you want to influence people, don't tell them who is boss. Even if you can get someone to do what you want because you are in a position of power, they'll either quit doing it when you're not around or they will refrain from innovating and asking questions that could benefit your business.*

- *Values are one of the strongest ways you can influence someone, according to experts. Therefore, if you want to make a request of an organization or an individual, it is helpful to understand what they hold as important and focus on highlighting how what you are asking for aligns with those values. In this way, you have a better chance of their accepting your ideas.*

- *Salespeople, perhaps more than any other profession, rely on their powers of persuasion to make a living and therefore are always coming up with innovative ways to serve their customers better. If you want some tips on how to be more persuasive, read some books on selling.*

- *Never leave a complaint unanswered. Often large institutions simply leave complaints received by letter or email unanswered in the hope that the problem will simply go away. Rather than taking complaints as a negative, think of each one as an opportunity to review and improve your operations.*

CHAPTER FIVE

Opening the Lines of Communication

Strategies to Help Reduce Misunderstandings and Encourage Positive Interaction

Try to win, and still more to deserve, the confidence of those with whom you are brought into contact. Many a man has owed his influence far more to character than to ability.

This is a story that for the longest time had a beginning and middle, but no definitive ending. For a long time, I used to tell the incomplete story. But with an ending, it became much better.

A couple of years ago, I was asked to be the master of ceremonies for a very posh event that had sold out the ballroom of a large Vancouver hotel. More than 1,000 people would be there and they expected a first-class act.

What would I wear? It's not a question one has to ask too often, but when it comes to presentation, there is always a choice. In this case, there was no doubt at all that I would be wearing a tuxedo. It went with the evening — a dash of fashion formality inevitably adds a little extra when the occasion is special.

As it was, I knew that I had a tux and all of the trimmings in my closet, but I hadn't worn it for some time and when I checked on the day of the event, I discovered that I had no matching black shoes. In fact, after a thorough examination of my wardrobe, I discovered that I had absolutely nothing in the way of footwear to match the elegance of the tuxedo. There were sandals, sneakers and battered brown brogues, but nothing in complementary black.

Thankfully, there was still time to fix the problem and during the course of my business day, I walked into a very prominent shoe store in downtown Vancouver and told the clerk, who on that occasion also happened to be the manager, of my predicament.

"No problem," he said, as he started measuring my foot, "we'll get you squared away in no time."

You should know that the name of the company was and is Sheppard Shoes, a retailer of considerable reputation in Vancouver. The name is important to the story. I will also let you know that the quoted price on the shoes being offered to me that day was $350! For a pair of shoes, it seemed like a fortune, but being frantic or perhaps a bit foolish, I agreed to the price.

It appeared that I was making progress . . . until the clerk informed me of a small problem.

The shoes I wanted weren't in stock at that store.

However, following a quick phone call, it was determined that they were in stock at Sheppard's second store several blocks away and it was suggested that I head on over there to pick them up myself.

Now, your expectations in life may be different from mine, but when I heard that bit of news from the man at Sheppard's, I was very disappointed. Having just said yes to a $350 pair of shoes, and having expressed concern about the limits on my time, I figured that Sheppard's might offer to have one of their people bring the shoes to me. The way I look at it, that's what customer service is all about. And besides, having someone bring the shoes would mean that while I was waiting for them to arrive, Sheppard's staff would have a perfect opportunity to offer me additional merchandise. I was already identified as a mark! More shoes, laces, socks, polish . . . even the store?

Apparently it hadn't occurred to the manager or anyone else on duty that once I'd left Sheppard's to make the long trek to their second store, that maybe a competitor's store across the street or down the block might catch my eye and they would lose the sale.

As it was, I didn't show that I was upset or make demands. I simply walked to the second store, paid my $350 and left with my new shoes (I was a smash hit at the big dinner, by the way).

But the story didn't end there. Like so many other dissatisfied customers, I began to share my story. However, unlike most others, I happen to make my living as a public speaker and therefore I've told thousands of people about those shoes and what I perceived as an example of less-than-great service. It was a cycle that may never have ended, except for the fact that one day I found the ending to the story sitting right in front of me in the audience at a speaking engagement. He introduced himself as the man who ran Sheppard Shoes.

Having heard my story, he was visibly upset, but he desperately wanted to make amends. He told me that he would follow up on my complaint, that in future there would be a clear understanding by the Sheppard's people about service, about pampering customers, about the importance of setting and meeting standards of customer satisfaction.

I'm happy to say that he was as good as his word. No one was fired, because it didn't require that kind of action, but the message was clear and the personal follow-up was as much — or more — than I could have expected.

And that was almost the ending of the story.

Except that the man who runs Sheppard's asked one thing of me in return. He requested that if I ever told the shoe story again, could I please add that he and the Sheppard's people had corrected the situation and to let people know that the story had a happy ending. I said I would, and I have.

Every customer in the world, whether they are buying shoes, ships or sealing wax, has an expectation of service. And even though standards of service should always be uniformly high, it's human nature for us to expect more service when we're spending more money.

It may be a funny quirk of human nature, but most of the time when service is bad, we don't tell the person who served us. We simply don't come back, and what's worse for the person or company that served us, is that we keep telling and retelling the story about the bad service we received. And those we tell, will tell others, and in due course hundreds or possibly even thousands of people hear about it. And in every retelling it gets worse!

You never know about customers. That's why we must always respect them for the heaven-sent treasures they are. It is that unique one-on-one relationship, no matter what you do, that will, at the very least, maintain your business, and at most, build your business.

I have walked many miles in my black shoes. They were ridiculously expensive, but they are also shoes of great quality and superb comfort. I thank the Sheppard's people for finding them for me — and for giving me the happy ending that makes the story worth telling over and over again.

OPENING THE LINES OF COMMUNICATION

As in the story I have just related to you, many of the problems that we encounter during our day-to-day interactions with others, both at home and in the workplace, are the result of poor communication. And often, when communication breaks down, it is because too much has been assumed by one or both parties.

Breakdowns can also result when the flow of information is in only one direction. When people perceive that they do not have an opportunity to respond or be heard, especially if they do not agree with what they are being told to do, they become less willing to cooperate and in some cases will even find ways to sabotage.

Good communication is essential to building trust between people and that requires a two-way dialogue. Ensuring that information is flowing in both directions helps to guarantee that people not only know what is expected of them and from them, but it also lets them know that their own contribution is valued.

Unfortunately, when it comes to improving communication, we often take a backwards approach. Instead of modelling good communication skills and mentoring those around us, we wait until someone makes a mistake and then chastise or correct them.

Imagine if your driving instructor had used this approach in teaching you how to drive a car. First, they'd put you in a manual-transmission car with no training and then they'd turn on the engine and shove the car into the street, expecting you to learn to drive based on the helpful suggestions yelled at you by other drivers.

Although criticism may have its place in identifying problems that need attention, as Sir John Lubbock pointed out in his book *Tact*, it should be reserved for private situations only.

"It never pays to criticize one employee in the presence of another," wrote Lubbock. "It may be all right — at times it may even be advantageous — to speak words of praise for other ears, but this is never true of criticism."

Wherever possible, it is much more advisable to be proactive rather than reactive in your approach. There are many positive ways to open the lines of communication in a work environment to encourage engagement and interaction. Some examples include:

- one-on-one meetings, staff meetings, group meetings and teleconferences;

- memos, reports, email, employee surveys, a suggestion box, newsletters, brochures;

- posters, videos, DVDs, screensavers, internal websites;

- informal chats, daily office walkabouts, social/community events, staff events to celebrate successes and milestones.

To open the lines of communication is to challenge yourself to look at things differently and to cultivate the ability to turn a problem into an opportunity for positive interaction. I had the chance to do just that during a recent speaking engagement.

In April of this year, I was invited to speak at the H.Y. Louie Company Ltd. study tour in Washington, D.C. Among their other business interests, the company owns all of the Marketplace IGA supermarkets in British Columbia. Over the years, I have had the privilege of speaking to this group in locations ranging from Scotland to Vienna, Bangkok, Hong Kong, Hawaii, Bermuda and Germany. Each trip is memorable for its cultural experience, but this trip ended up being memorable for another reason.

To take their B.C. delegates to Washington, the company chartered an airplane from Omni Air International, based out of Tulsa, Oklahoma. The flight was direct from Vancouver to Washington. Therefore, we cleared customs in Vancouver and at the same time, checked our bags through to Washington. On further investigation, I found that Omni Air doesn't do these charters too often. If you've never heard of Omni Air, you're not alone. That's because they don't actually do a lot of charters of any kind.

Omni has a contract with the U.S. government and most of their flights entail the transfer of military troops from Baltimore to Iraq. Nevertheless, the aircraft was modern with good food and friendly service, which made for an uneventful journey — as someone who doesn't like high-altitude surprises, the fact that it was uneventful made it a great flight in my book.

We arrived at Baltimore International Airport and wouldn't you know, my luggage did not arrive with that of the other 249 passengers. As I stood there contemplating the situation, I wondered if my suitcase had somehow stayed on the plane and would eventually find its way to Iraq . . . where someone would be walking the streets of Baghdad in my Harry Rosen suit.

Realizing that there was nothing more to wait for, my wife Kay and I filled out the necessary forms for missing luggage and then joined the delegates for the bus trip to our hotel. On the ride in from the airport, news of my missing luggage spread through the group and everyone was sympathetic. After all, two days from then, I was supposed to get up in front of everyone to deliver my speech and I had no suit, no tie and no dress shirt or shoes. In fact, I had nothing except the clothes on my back.

We arrived at the Willard InterContinental hotel in Washington, D.C., on Pennsylvania Avenue. It's a splendid hotel just two blocks from the White House. We got our room key and didn't have to waste any time unpacking.

It was about 10 o'clock on a Sunday evening and the weather was spectacular and so warm, even at that time of night. Kay and I went downstairs to the concierge, Jeffrey Hlaing, and told him about the missing luggage and my predicament.

"I absolutely have to have a suit for my presentation on Wednesday morning," I told him. "Any recommendations?"

The concierge told us that there was only one person in Washington who could do this on time. His name was Georges De Paris and he just happened to be the tailor to the U.S. president. In fact, he created the blue ties that President George W. Bush wears on camera and his custom tailoring shop was literally half a block from the hotel. Just one small problem, it was Sunday night and the shop was closed. The concierge recommended that we go to see Georges first thing in the morning.

"Let's wander up there and see if we can locate the shop so we'll know where we're going in the morning," I suggested to Kay, given that it was a warm spring evening and we had nothing better to do.

Before we left the concierge, he told me that Georges was a very eccentric fellow.

"In fact," he said, "he's quite a character."

So we strolled up the street to Georges's store on a balmy Sunday evening in Washington. As it turned out, Georges Ladies and Men's Custom Tailoring Shop was very easy to find. We were told that Georges De Paris was a master designer with French and German diplomas, who speaks English, French, Spanish, German, Italian and

Greek. With a background like that, it's a surprise that he went into tailoring rather than taking a post with the United Nations.

Kay and I pressed our noses against the window, trying to get a peek into the deserted shop and before heading back to the hotel, agreed to come back first thing in the morning. However, as we turned to walk away, a character, who could have been Buddy Hackett or maybe even Albert Einstein, suddenly popped up from out of nowhere on the other side of the glass and beckoned us into the shop. He met us at the door wearing just one shoe with his fly undone and the tail of his shirt sticking out through the zipper. Interestingly, he was completely oblivious to his dishevelled state of dress and was, instead, interested to know what we needed.

We explained the situation with our missing luggage and how I was the speaker at a conference and in need of a suit, shirt and tie, ready for Wednesday morning. In response, he mentioned that he made the blue ties that George Bush wears when he is on camera and added as an afterthought that the President only wore the blue ties when he was in a good mood. Georges then proceeded to begin fitting me for a suit that he assured me would be ready for Wednesday.

"How much?" I inquired.

"Only $2,000 U.S.," came the answer, which was somewhat more than I wanted to pay given that I was anticipating my luggage would arrive before Wednesday morning. Not knowing what other options I might have to get a suit, I told him I would be back in the morning.

At breakfast on Monday morning, everyone was curious to know if I had received my luggage. I told them there was still no sign of the suitcase, but the airline assured me that they were tracking it down.

At this point, I was starting to think, "How am I to deal with the inconvenience of having no luggage for the week and how will my response and mood be perceived by the convention delegates?" Thinking about my predicament I was reminded of a comment from Oprah Winfrey about cultivating gratitude:

"Keep a grateful journal," she encouraged. "And every night list five things that happened that day that you are grateful for. What it will begin to do is change your perspective on your day and your life. If you can learn to focus on what you have, you will always see that the universe is abundant and you will have more. If you concentrate on what you don't have, you will never have enough."

It seemed to me that my next actions were on full display and therefore, tact in the way I handled the situation was paramount. Yes, I had lost my luggage; yes, it was inconvenient and yes, it was frustrating, but on reflection, my wife and I (and the entire planeload of delegates) had arrived without incident after a five-and-a-half-hour journey. Therefore, all that I had really lost were some clothes that were easy enough to replace. That's it. Putting it into perspective, it wasn't much of an inconvenience.

I cheered up and enjoyed the company around me as I ate.

After finishing our breakfast, my wife and I ventured out of the hotel only to discover a Macy's department store not a block from the hotel. We entered the store with enthusiasm and later that day, I was back in business with a new suit, tie and shirt — tailored for less than $300! As it turned out, Macy's was having one of their giant sales that day. To make it even better, I returned to the store with my Canadian passport some days later and received an additional 11 per cent off.

If you hadn't already guessed, I used my lost luggage adventure as my opening story at the conference on Wednesday morning and I do believe the point about staying focused on what is important and being grateful for what we have rather than what we don't made an impression on the audience.

I also called Georges De Paris to let him know that $2,000 was more than I wanted to spend on a suit; however, I'm happy to report that many of the delegates from the conference paid him a visit to buy some of his famous blue ties.

In the end, my missing luggage did manage to turn up in my room the day before I was to leave Washington for the next leg of my journey, although by that point I had replaced most of what I needed so its return was somewhat anticlimactic. More importantly, I realized that no matter what I think or feel in a given situation, it's how and what I choose to communicate to those around me that influence the real outcome. I can focus on the negative and let it drag me down, or I can focus on the positive and encourage others to do the same. We all must take responsibility for how our behaviour affects the people around us. If we allow ourselves to get sidetracked by small concerns, we will ultimately create problems for ourselves. However, if we take the time to put the situation in perspective and choose to work with what we have, that which appeared to be a problem can be turned into an opportunity.

When I returned home in May, I sent the following letter to Omni Air:

May 4, 2007

Omni Air International
Attention: LaDonna Brauchle

Dear LaDonna,

It was a pleasure to have the opportunity to fly with Omni Air International on the charter from Vancouver to Baltimore on April 22 with the H.Y. Louie Company Ltd. (Marketplace IGA group).

The flight attendants were exceptional and the customer service was outstanding. I can see why your airline is a big hit with the U.S. troops that you frequently take to Iraq.

As you are aware, I was the individual whose luggage went astray for almost the entire convention. Given the fact that I was one of the guest speakers on Wednesday, April 25, I was required to purchase virtually an entire wardrobe just for that occasion.

Hansi from Pro Tours has indicated that you may be willing to reimburse me for the costs incurred. To that end, please find attached a receipt from Macy's for $510.59 USD and a *copy of the lost/delay report.*

If you have any questions or require additional information, please contact my assistant, Dale Clarke.

Thank you very much for your assistance.

Kind regards,

Peter Legge
President
Peter Legge Management Company Ltd.

I'm happy to report that within seven days of sending the letter, I received a response back from Omni Air, along with a cheque that fully refunded the money I had spent to replace my lost possessions. That's what I call good customer service. I could have yelled at Ms. Brauchle, but she wasn't the one who lost my luggage, and she was the person who could authorize the cheque, which she did. Do you think the tone and tact of this letter helped her to make the decision as to whether or not to reimburse my money? And now, this story has found its way into one of my books, which will be read by hundreds of thousands of people. Would you be willing to pay $500 to have the same thing said about your company? It's something to think about the next time you handle a customer complaint. In the end, it costs very little to be tactful, but it can make a world of difference.

WHEN OPENING THE LINES OF COMMUNICATION ISN'T ENOUGH

If you feel you have done all that you can to open the lines of communication and it hasn't had the desired result, consider this advice from Sir John Lubbock, "It is important to choose well those who are to work with you, and under you; to put the square man in the square hole and the round man in the round hole."

In other words, don't expect people to change the essence of who they are in order to fit the circumstances. Rather, identify and build on the strengths that they have.

TACTICAL MANOEUVRES

- *Many people have the potential to contribute in a significant way; they need only encouragement to develop.*

- *Never chastise an employee for what they have not done in the past. Compliment and thank them for what they have done. Also, tell them that you know they can do a great deal better, and that you want to help them.*

- *Everyone appreciates being recognized as a human being, rather than simply as a means through which their employer is able to generate profit. Simply approaching your employees with a pleasant attitude can affect the work environment in a positive way as others take their cue from you. As we all know, enthusiasm is contagious and the creation of an environment where work is an enjoyable activity will go a long way towards boosting both morale and productivity.*

- *Develop your staff's people skills. People skills constitute 85 per cent of your success in business, as in life. If the quality of relations between you and your customer is paramount, spend the time and effort to teach your employees how to make every encounter a positive experience.*

- *Tell others what you* can *do for them. Nobody wants to hear what you* can't *do. Offer one or more solutions to a problem and then make sure you get agreement from the other party before you move on.*

- *Be available when others need you.*

- *Be sensitive to body language and other cues. Not every person communicates dissatisfaction in words. You need to be tuned in to non-verbal clues as well. If you don't feel your message is being received, ask questions or try taking a different approach. Be aware of the person who doesn't complain but also doesn't take an active role in discussions. It all comes back to the quality of communication.*

- *When you get positive feedback on a staff member's performance, share it with everyone. Recognition and rewards are also great ways to thank employees and to inspire the whole team to achieve more.*

CHAPTER SIX

Conflict Resolution

Why Listening Skills Are Critical to the Problem-solving Process

It is far easier to read books than people. In this, the eyes are a great guide. When the eyes say one thing and the tongue another, a wise person relies on the language of the first.

Holding onto anger is like grasping a hot coal with the intent of throwing it at someone else; you are the one getting burned. These are the wise words of Buddha.

Most of us have to deal with conflict in some form

every day. Whether we find ourselves in the midst of a disagreement with a colleague or client, or dealing with a misunderstanding between family members, friends or neighbours, it's difficult to separate the emotions from the real issues. However, contrary to what you might think, conflicts don't need to be volatile and negative.

It's how we deal with conflict that determines the outcome. As long as you approach the situation with the right attitude, conflicts can actually result in a positive experience that leads to increased understanding and an atmosphere that promotes creative problem solving. Learning and using conflict resolution skills can allow you to take a step back, breathe deeply and really listen to the views and needs of others. The more you practise these skills, the easier it will become to solve problems.

Here are some guidelines (based on methods taken from the fields of diplomacy and counselling) that can help you deal with any type of conflict that may arise in your life:

Step 1. *Deal effectively with your anger and take time to cool off.*
Conflicts can't be solved in the face of hot emotions. You can't negotiate a resolution if you and/or the other person are too angry to think straight, or if you don't acknowledge your feelings. Therefore, take a step back, breathe deeply and gain some emotional distance before trying to talk things out. This way you can choose your response rather than simply reacting out of anger.

I had to do just that during a recent managers' meeting at my own company, Canada Wide Media Limited. Rather than letting loose and saying something that I might regret later, I excused myself to get a cup of coffee and took those few minutes to get my emotions in check. When I returned to the meeting, I was feeling much more rational and we were able to deal with the situation in a constructive way.

If you need a distraction to help you cool down, consider: breathing deeply while making a calming statement to yourself, taking a short walk, clearing your desk or straightening up something in the room, splashing cold water on your face or writing in a journal before coming back to talk about the problem. Some people need a physical release, while others need something to calm their mind. Find out what works best for you and try it the next time you get angry. Then you'll be ready to move on to the next step.

Step 2. *Set a positive tone.*
Invite the other person to talk or negotiate and state positive intentions, such as, "I'd like to make things better between us," or "It's important for me to understand your point of view." Acknowledge and validate the other person's effort with a positive statement such as: "I can see this is difficult for you also," or "Thank you for working with me on this."

Step 3. *Discuss and define the problem.*
"I" messages can be useful in allowing you to express how you feel without attacking or blaming. By starting with "I" you take responsibility for the way you perceive the problem. This is in sharp contrast to "you" messages, which can put others on the defensive and often slam the door on further communication.

A statement like, "You took all of the easy job orders and left me with the difficult ones! Don't you ever think of anyone but yourself?" will likely escalate the conflict. Whereas, "I'm annoyed because I thought we agreed that we would alternate taking incoming orders to ensure that they were fairly distributed" delivers a far less aggressive and judgemental message.

When discussing the problem, it's important to avoid put-downs, guilt-trips, sarcasm or negative body language. The objective is to be non-combative and willing to compromise. A main belief of conflict resolution is, "It's us against the problem, not us against each other." "I" messages allow you to convey this.

Step 4. *Listen and reflect.*
Each person takes a turn to restate what they heard the other person say. Reflective listening demonstrates that we care enough to hear the other person out, rather than just focusing on our own point of view. It actually fosters empathy.

Step 5. *Take responsibility.*
In the majority of conflicts, both parties have some degree of responsibility. However, most of us tend to blame rather than looking at our own role in the problem. When we take responsibility we shift the conflict into an entirely different gear, one where resolution is possible.

Step 6. *Brainstorm solutions and come up with one that satisfies both parties.*
Resolving conflicts is a creative act. There are many solu-

tions to a single problem. The key is a willingness to seek compromises. Brainstorming is a way to turn the focus away from each other and onto the problem, which opens both parties up to new possibilities. A lasting solution will address the main interests of both parties.

Step 7. *Acknowledge, forgive or thank.*
Simply acknowledging the other person's willingness to work things out at the end of a conflict sends a message of conciliation and gratitude. It's an important step that can preserve the relationship and strengthen connections making it easier to work through problems that may arise in the future.

When things get heated, conflict resolution skills can be used in every aspect of life. However, being quick in your response to resolve issues can go a long way towards avoiding conflict in the first place. If you identify a problem or one is brought to your attention, you need to deal with it immediately. Here is a good example of what I'm talking about.

On entering a hotel room, a guest commented to her husband that there was a stain on the chair where she had intended to lay her coat. The bellman immediately left and returned with a housekeeping staff member, who quickly cleaned the spot. It was an action that both satisfied the guest (averting a possible complaint to the manager or worse yet, a story about the hotel that the guest would repeat time and again to friends and acquaintances) and delivered the clear message that the hotel was truly dedicated to serving the needs of the guest.

Don't be fooled into thinking that a small concern, like the one just mentioned, won't turn into a bigger problem. The best time to resolve any conflict is when it is still a small matter.

As the saying goes, "It's the little things that count." It's also the little things that can build up into big things before you know it, especially when pride and ego come into the picture.

Just as importantly, when people are coming to you for help to solve a problem, don't rush them, but give the situation the time and attention it deserves. That way, you will be more likely to come up with the best solution rather than just a quick fix. In addition, a big part of conflict resolution is giving people the chance to be heard. Often, just having the opportunity to talk about the problem without being challenged or interrupted can help to defuse someone's anger and frustration to a level where they are in a better frame of mind to come up with possible solutions.

"Argument is always a little dangerous," said Sir John Lubbock. "It often leads to coolness and misunderstandings. You may gain your argument and lose your friend, which is probably a bad bargain." But how do you deal with a problem without turning it into an argument? When addressing a problem or conflict, if you work from the viewpoint of people's strengths and abilities rather than their weaknesses, you will automatically be attuned to the positive possibilities within them, and more often than not, you will find that they rise to the occasion.

This approach is something that has worked well in my own business. For example, I know that the people I have hired to work with me at Canada Wide are intelligent, competent and capable individuals. That's the reason I hired them in the first place. Therefore, whenever a conflict is brought to my attention where a manager or employee has made a decision that, on the surface, I don't agree with or can't see the logic in, I resist the temptation to overrule their decision or be confrontational. Instead, I say, "I'm not sure how you arrived at your decision. Can you take me through it and explain how you came to this conclusion?"

Very often, by simply taking the time to let them walk me through their decision-making process, I will discover a fact or circumstance that completely changes the context of the situation and that new information helps me to see their logic, which in turn, simply reaffirms my confidence in their abilities.

As business owners and entrepreneurs, we can often get caught up in believing that our way of thinking or doing is the best way and we can lose sight of the fact that other approaches can be just as effective in reaching the end goal. And if in the process of reaching that goal, employees and managers are given the freedom to stretch their abilities — and sometimes fail — imagine how much more they will be able to contribute to their various endeavours.

As well-meaning as our interference can be, it is also counterproductive to our purpose, just as the red tape and endless documentation required by governments and large corporations can be counterproductive to making business run more smoothly. Parents, too, often interfere unnecessarily in their children's lives.

Look before you leap.

It never hurts to examine the likely outcome of your words or actions before taking them. Being able to put your ego on hold for long enough to consider that your interference in the affairs of others may lead to negative outcomes is a useful thing. Also, consider that sometimes it's better to do nothing. It's a hard lesson to swallow, but one that ultimately leads to more successful results.

TACTICAL MANOEUVRES

- *Often, people criticize without referring to an underlying conflict. If you don't figure out what the real conflict is, you'll never be able to resolve it. Try to focus your comments on the problem, not the personalities involved.*

- *Letting negative feelings build up inside isn't healthy. If you find this happening, seek out an opportunity to tell those involved in the situation how you are feeling. Whether you are upset, annoyed or enraged, unless you communicate, it is unlikely that others will pick up on what is really going on. More likely, you will simply develop a reputation as someone who is sullen or difficult. Remember, sometimes the offence is unintentional and simply bringing it to the attention of the other person can ensure that it doesn't happen again.*

- *During a conflict, give and request feedback. Use open-ended questions to encourage the other person to share their concerns.*

- *If it's your turn to listen, avoid interrupting with defensive remarks. When people feel they aren't being heard, they will only come on stronger.*

- *If you believe you're being lied to, before accusing, ask the person some questions and attempt to discern what is true or false.*

- *Do you find yourself in one conflict after another? Pay attention to the circumstances that are leading to conflict, and you might discover that what's going on is a personality clash rather than a conflict over substantial issues.*

- *If you find yourself in a situation where you can't keep your cool, ask for the meeting to be rescheduled so that you can listen without losing your temper.*

- *If you find yourself overreacting to the criticism of others in a conflict situation, it's usually because you're afraid of losing something. What is it? Are your fears valid?*

- *If you encounter conflict frequently, you may find that the stress is making you vulnerable. Consider counselling, or try using visualization, exercise, aromatherapy or other stress-management devices to relieve the stress.*

- *No matter what anyone says, it is never easy to take criticism, even if the criticism is positive, constructive and delivered with the utmost tact. Here are some helpful hints on how to take the heat.*

1. *Show the person doing the criticizing that you have heard his or her criticism by pausing, nodding or giving*

some sort of verbal acknowledgment.

2. *Ask for more information about the criticizer's comments to give both of you some time to cool down. Try to look for the criticizer's positive intent.*

3. *Respond to the criticism by sharing your perspective on the situation, but do so in a calm manner. If the other person is agitated, hopefully this will encourage them to calm down, too. After all, it would be embarrassing for them to lose their cool while you remain composed.*

4. *Listen for commonalities between your perspective and that of your critic and try to build from them.*

5. *Ask for feedback on your viewpoint.*

6. *If you feel that they have misunderstood your perspective, try rephrasing your ideas.*

7. *Demonstrate your desire to find a compromise. Try to determine what the criticizer's real objection is to your behaviour and consider how you can solve it. Ask if he or she has a solution in mind.*

8. *If you find that you aren't able to come to a resolution, remember that you can't always please everyone. Ask yourself whether there's truth in your critic's complaints, or whether this may be someone you just can't make happy. If it's the latter, perhaps you should consider minimizing your contact with this person in the future (if possible).*

CHAPTER SEVEN

Negotiation

How Your Communication Style Determines What You Get

What we see depends mainly on what we look for.

"Till death us do part."

It's a phrase of enormous finality, but if you are married, you probably included it as one of the promises you made on your wedding day.

To have and to hold, in sickness and in health . . . till death us do part. With the best of intentions, in surroundings that always add great weight and solemnity to the vows, we commit to live life together. Forever.

Sometimes it works.

My first and only wife Kay and I celebrate our 40th wedding anniversary this year.

There have been some exceptional moments in our marriage. Thankfully, my wife has been able to accompany me as I travelled to many of my speaking engagements and charity commitments around the globe and we have had quite a few adventures as a result. However, there have also been many times when the Legge marriage has been considerably less than a bed of roses. Like any union, there have been lots of ups, downs and uncertain moments that severely tested the sincerity of our promises.

But till death us do part has meant exactly that for Kay and me. We always work things out and keep on going — because way back in our early days, we saw something in each other that lit a fire we believed could burn for a lifetime.

I was virtually flat broke when we were married in England. Eight English pounds was all I had to buy Kay's wedding ring — by any standards, not a lot of money, even back then. But it was a ring that was bright, shiny and made of gold.

When the minister said: "You may put the ring on Kay's finger," it didn't slip on all that easily. But it did go on and found its place comfortably on the third finger of her left hand.

No matter what anyone else might have thought, to both Kay and myself, it looked quite marvellous. We smiled at each other and knew that the ring was indeed a shining symbol of a life together that for us was beginning at that moment.

Over the years, I believe that inexpensive wedding ring has become my wife's most cherished possession. It has some visible nicks and scratches, the kind of bumps and wear that time gives to most everything. On the surface, the lustre of the metal is less than it was on the day we were married. But the inside of the ring has grown smoother, as has our marriage over those 40 years. In fact, Kay says that the ring fits better today than it did on our wedding day. Like our relationship, it has moulded itself into something closer, something finer and more precious to us both.

The De Beers people say that somewhere along the way in a relationship, we should all be buying the big diamonds we couldn't afford when we were courting. But those of us who are truly sharing our lives together give in other ways, and we do it every day. Not with diamonds, but with smiles, kindness, words of reassurance, touching and caring. And for us, the small, inexpensive band of gold at the centre of all of this still works extremely well. Over the years its value has appreciated far beyond mere money. Its value is up there almost beyond understanding.

Life *is* commitment. It's making promises to ourselves and to others and keeping them . . . to our wives and husbands, our children, our extended families. It's commitments in business, the way we *do* business, and how we treat those whom we serve in business.

Working things out within the parameters of "till death us do part" and other commitments often requires compromise and a willingness to negotiate. Negotiation is a part of life with which we all have to deal. Being able to negotiate well can make a big difference in how we get along with others and how satisfied we are with life. Although many people will tell you that a shrewd negotiator is someone who can make a good deal for themselves without having to give much in return, I would use another word to describe such a person. In business as in marriage, parenting and everything else, if you're only in it for what *you* can get, even if you eventually make it to the top, you're going to be very lonely (and insecure) when you get there.

Here are some tactful strategies to keep in mind as you negotiate your way through life.

Be willing to negotiate in the first place

There is no point in going to the negotiation table if you're too angry or frustrated to think straight or if you've already made up your mind that it is "your way or the highway." To negotiate in good faith, you must first be willing and able to participate in a discussion about the interests and objectives of both sides before you can consider looking for a possible solution. If you're not there yet, take some time to think over your options or find a neutral third party to talk it over with. Often, simply allowing yourself a day or two to vent your feelings before attempting to negotiate can help to put the situation in perspective.

Don't get emotionally tied up in winning

One big mistake many people make when negotiating is that they get too emotionally invested in winning. Often they will shout, make demands or even threaten in order to get their way. Not only is this behaviour counterproductive to the negotiation process, it's also far from tactful.

Often, an agreement is only possible if both people involved feel that they're getting something out of it. If the person across the table feels attacked, or doesn't like you, they probably won't be willing to make concessions and they are much more likely to walk away from the deal altogether. A lot of people hate bullies, and will be more willing to walk away from a transaction if it involves one.

Try to remain calm, patient and responsive throughout the negotiation process, even if the other person starts to lose their cool. Park your ego at the door and leave it there, and you'll have a much better chance of succeeding.

A successful negotiator finds out what the needs of the other party are and tries to meet them without losing sight of his own goals.

Focus on the benefits for the other party
Just like you, the other party in the negotiation is wondering what's in it for them if they give you what you are asking for. By making sure that there is a benefit for them (and that you've clearly stated what it is), you will be that much closer to an agreement.

A matter of dollars and sense
Negotiating for money is difficult for many of us. That's because we often equate our own worth with how much

of it we have or how much we are able to get. When it comes to bidding or offering, the best advice I can give is "do your homework ahead of time so that you know what is a fair price going in." If price is an issue for you, get at least two other quotes or appraisals before you start to negotiate.

If you feel too much pressure, it's okay to defer authority
If you find yourself in the position of negotiating with someone who is relentless in their approach, don't allow yourself to be bullied. Even if you can't take them on yourself, you can still defer authority by saying something like, "Well, I'll have to talk it over with my spouse/boss/business partner before I can give you a definite yes."

This gives you time to go away and think through your position (based on the facts of the situation, rather than the pressure of the moment) in order to make the best decision for you. It's also a great strategy for preventing people from rushing you.

Don't leave the other person feeling as if they've been manipulated
Many people make the mistake of trying to squeeze every last drop of benefit out of every negotiation they are involved in. However, if the other person feels that they've been manipulated, or worse yet, cheated, they may not follow through on their part of the deal, or they may just refuse to deal with you in the future.

Whenever possible, a negotiation should leave both parties feeling satisfied with the outcome. Be willing to give up things that don't really matter to you in order to create a feeling of goodwill. For example, if you're negotiating for a lower rate on a lease agreement, offer to sign a slightly longer term in exchange for the lower rate. That way, both parties receive a benefit and there is plenty of goodwill for future negotiations.

Never cut what you can untie.
— Joseph Joubert

Here are some more tips to keep in mind when you are negotiating:

- Choose an appropriate time and location for the negotiation. Consider meeting in a neutral place.

- Make sure that you are not going to be disturbed or feel rushed.

- Think about what you want to say prior to the negotiation and make a note of important points.

- Also think about how you will respond/deal with possible counterpoints in the negotiation.

- To begin, outline and present the problem/issue in a constructive way.

- Be specific about what you are negotiating and focus on that; don't bring in other issues or concerns.

- Stay focused on the subject of negotiation throughout the process.

- Only interrupt the negotiation to take a break if either of you becomes over-emotional.

- Allow equal time for yourself and the other party to present positions and possible solutions.

- Listening does not imply that you agree, so don't interrupt constantly with counter arguments. Wait for your turn and then counter.

- From time to time, summarize what you have heard in your own words to check that you understand what the other party is saying. Summarizing lets the other party know that you have paid attention.

- If you are negotiating a change in behaviour, use just a few examples to illustrate.

- Accept the fact that you cannot have it all your way and be prepared to compromise.

- Tell the other party what you are willing to give up in order to reach an agreement.

"Be wary and keep cool," advised Sir John Lubbock. "A cool head is as necessary as a warm heart. In any negotiations, steadiness and coolness are invaluable. While they will often carry you in safety through times of danger and difficulty, nothing is improved by anger."

TACTICAL MANOEUVRES

- *"Roughness is not strength," said Sir John Lubbock. "It is indeed often the cloak of weakness. If it is necessary to find fault, at least speak kindly." Tact is often the spoonful of sugar that helps the medicine go down. None of us likes to have our shortcomings pointed out, however necessary it might be to address them. Therefore, if you really want someone else to change their behaviour, consider how you would like to be addressed if the tables were turned and act accordingly.*

- *Take time to prepare. This is the most important step in many negotiations. You want to be as thoroughly informed as possible before you open your mouth.*

- *Sir John also recommended patience. "In any business or negotiations, be patient," he said in* Tact. *"Many a man would rather you heard his story than granted his request; many an opponent has been tired out. Whatever you do, do it well."*

- *Never disrespect others, even if you're right. When people feel disrespected they become more rigid and are likely to withhold information that is important to the negotiation. It's easy to let frustration, anger or resent-*

ment cloud your judgement, but no matter what, don't snap. Remember, it takes years to build up a reputation and only seconds to destroy it. If you find yourself getting emotional, excuse yourself and get a glass of water or take a quick walk to calm down before proceeding.

- *Don't attribute your motives to other people. It is not unusual to go into a negotiation and assume that any other intelligent person is going to think and feel the same way we do. Wrong. In many cases, people are strongly influenced by emotional factors that we have no knowledge of. That is why an important part of negotiating is listening to find out what the other party really wants.*

Chapter Eight

When the Going Gets Tough

Dealing With Difficult People

Do not make enemies for yourself, you can make nothing worse.

In my previous book, *If Only I'd Said That: Volume IV*, I discussed the global strategy and technology consulting firm, Booz Allen Hamilton, which wanted to discover why some institutions endure for decades or even centuries, while others disappear into history. They defined an enduring institution as "one that has changed and grown in unswerving pursuit of success and relevance, yet remained true throughout time to its founding principles."

To complete its task, the firm asked leading scholars at

respected universities across the U.S. to nominate institutions that have adapted, endured and prevailed, standing the test of time and successfully reinventing themselves to meet the changing conditions.

Eventually, they came up with a list of the top 10:

1. Oxford University

2. The Olympic Games

3. The Rolling Stones

4. The American Constitution

5. Dartmouth College

6. General Electric

7. Sony

8. International Telecommunications Union

9. The Rockefeller Foundation

10. The Salvation Army

If you don't know the history of the organization, you might be surprised to see The Salvation Army on that list, but I'm not. William Booth, founder of The Salvation Army, started his fledgling organization in 1865 as an evangelistic ministry to the poor and downtrodden of London's

Eastside, but his first few years of work were little more than struggle and suffering.

At the age of 13, William, who had grown up in a household without enough money to have him schooled, was sent out to learn a trade. He was apprenticed to a pawnbroker in a seedy part of Nottingham, England.

"Make money," was the advice of Booth's father, who died bankrupt the following year.

Booth did learn about making money while learning his trade. But his apprenticeship also gave him another kind of education. Working in a pawnbroker's shop, he was in daily contact with the poor and destitute. It's no coincidence that during his years as an apprentice, he became a person of faith — a Christian.

In 1849, William Booth moved to London and took a position in a pawnshop in a poor area south of the Thames River. But after only three years, he gave up this trade and became a minister. He did so because he saw faith as the solution to the problems of those who were struggling to survive. As such, he embarked on a lifelong mission that had two just objectives: saving lost souls and righting social injustices.

At first he became a Methodist New Connexion minister and then a travelling evangelist. But in 1865, when some people from the area heard him preach in front of the Blind Beggar Pub in East London, he was recruited to become part of a tent ministry that came to be called the Christian Mission.

From there, Booth ministered to the poorest people in London. At that time, the East End contained half of the paupers, homeless and starving in the entire city. His early converts were some of the most desperate types of people; thieves, prostitutes, gamblers and drunkards.

Booth was trying to make a difference, but his efforts were not met with appreciation, even from the very people he was trying to help. He and his fellow workers were harassed and brutalized. Local tavern keepers worked especially hard to undermine his efforts. Even street children threw stones and fireworks through the window of their meeting hall, and Booth's wife, Catherine, said that he would "stumble home night after night, haggard with fatigue. Often his clothes were torn and bloody bandages swathed his head where a stone had struck." But Booth would not retaliate in kind. And he refused to give up. Instead, he worked to feed the poor, house the homeless and share his faith.

His organization continued to grow. By 1867, Booth had 10 full-time workers. By 1874, more than a thousand volunteers and 42 evangelists worked with him, and in 1878, when they reorganized, Booth gave the group a new name and The Salvation Army was born.

Unfortunately, that didn't stop the group's opponents. Booth was labelled "anti-Christ" by the reformer Lord Shaftesbury. An opposition group also formed to try to stop Booth and his associates, and they came to call themselves The Skeleton Army. The object of The Skeleton Army was to put down the Salvationists by following them about everywhere, beating a drum and burlesquing their songs, to render the conduct of their processions and services impossible.

Despite the horrible treatment they received, the officers and volunteers of The Salvation Army persevered, and they helped hundreds of thousands of people. Often, they converted the very individuals who had once persecuted them.

In 1912, William Booth, then age 83, delivered his last public address, and in it he stated his commitment to investing in people:

> While women weep — as they do now — I'll
> fight
> While little children go hungry — as they do
> now — I'll fight
> While men go to prison in and out, in and out
> as they do now — I'll fight
> While there is a drunkard left — I'll fight
> While there is a poor girl lost on the streets
> — I'll fight
> While there remains one dark soul without
> the light of God — I'll fight.
> I'll fight to the very end!

So how did this one man leave behind an organization so prepared for the future that it could continue growing strong nearly 100 years after his death, recently attracting the largest single charitable donation — $1.5 billion — in history?

Simple.

As Booth said, "We saw the need, we saw the people starving, we saw people going about half-naked, people doing sweated labour, and we set about bringing a remedy to these things. We were obliged. There was a compulsion. How could you do anything else?"

Indeed. Despite whatever opposition William Booth faced, he stayed true to his convictions and persevered in light of a greater purpose. Although we can be thankful that we don't face the magnitude of opposition that Booth did, we all come across difficult people in business and our personal lives, or at least people with behaviours that make them very difficult to deal with.

How many of these behaviours do you recognize?

Tyrants and Dictators
They're constantly demanding and brutally critical of everyone in their sphere of influence. They bully and intimidate everyone around them to get what they want.

Superstars and Power Junkies
They can't stand it when someone else is in the spotlight and they'll do anything to get the attention back on themselves, even if it means taking credit for the accomplishments of others.

Know-It-Alls
They're arrogant and generally feel a need to force others to listen to their opinion on every issue. When they're proven wrong or their ideas are challenged, they get angry and defensive.

Complainers

They complain constantly and their dismal outlook can poison the atmosphere around them. Although they may be smart and skilled, they prefer complaining to finding solutions.

Passives and Passive-Aggressives

Although they go through the motions at meetings, they never offer ideas or let you know where they stand. Worse, they appear to agree with plans and then simply go off and do whatever they like with no regard for how it will affect others.

Gossips

They relish other people's troubles and can't wait to share the news — even if it is "only a rumour."

Underminers

They have their own agenda and will pursue it no matter what the cost to those around them. When they offer information, you never know how much of it is true and they will often conceal information to manipulate others. They're never happier than when someone else's idea or project fails and they can say, "I told you so."

"Yes" People

They can never quite bring themselves to say

no, so they'll agree to almost anything, but rarely deliver on a commitment. You can never depend on them to follow through.

Dr. "No"
Offer an idea, and they'll immediately point out 10 reasons why it won't work. Worse, they rarely have ideas of their own and they're completely inflexible when it comes to modifying an idea to make it work.

Do you know how to work with these difficult behaviours?
Understanding how difficult people think, what they fear and why they do what they do can make dealing with them a lot less frustrating. Knowing how to deal with difficult behaviour at work will allow you to approach your job with more enjoyment and your business associates with greater confidence.

Why are some people just so difficult to deal with?
Although some people are intentionally destructive and hurtful, many others can appear to be difficult simply because we don't understand what motivates them to behave the way they do. Is it simply a matter of not having learned proper communication, social or conflict resolution skills? Surprisingly, more often than not, the answer is yes. Because these people don't perceive their behaviour as being anything out of the norm, they continue on, oblivious to the fact that their actions are having a negative impact on those around them.

Why avoidance and appeasement don't work when dealing with difficult people

An obvious way of dealing with difficult people is just to stay away from them. The problem with this approach is that you can't control everything around you. The energy you will waste in actively avoiding contact and the stress that results from constantly looking over your shoulder — particularly if the person is in your workplace or neighbourhood — make this a bad proposition on your part. More importantly, by avoiding the person and not learning to deal with the behaviour effectively, you are setting yourself up as someone who runs away from problems.

The same holds true for appeasement, or "giving in" to avoid conflict. Although it may be necessary from time to time to delay discussion to a more appropriate time or setting, as a strategy for dealing with someone who is controlling or bossy, it simply gives them permission to continue behaving badly. People who try to appease or please the difficult people around them often build up anger and resentment as a result of feeling powerless or victimized. Unfortunately, rather than direct that anger towards solving the problem, they eventually turn it inward on themselves as a punishment for being weak.

Change begins with you

It probably won't come as a big surprise to you that dealing with difficult people begins with dealing with yourself first. Your first line of defence against annoying behaviour of any kind is to address your own reaction. If you personalize the problem or get into blaming, you simply allow yourself to get drawn in. Focus instead on problem solving. You may not always be able to change the difficult behaviour of others, but you can change the way you react to it.

I devoted an entire chapter in *Make Your Life a Masterpiece* to this very subject. The chapter talks about how, as an individual, the kind of personality you develop can be your greatest asset or your greatest liability due to the fact that it entails everything that you control: mind, body and soul. It determines not just how others see you, but how you experience life as evidenced by the following story from *Masterpiece* about a city man who bought a farm:

On the first day that he arrived on his new farm, the city fellow went out to look at the fence around his property (which had been the source of much quarrelling for the previous owner). As he walked around the perimeter, the neighbouring farmer suddenly appeared and said to him, "That fence is a full foot over on my side."

"No problem," said the new owner, "We will set the fence two feet over on my side."

"Oh, but that's more than I claim," stammered the surprised farmer.

"Never mind about that; I would much rather have peace with my neighbour than two feet of earth," said the man.

"That's surely fine of you, sir," replied the farmer, "But I couldn't let you do a thing like that. That fence will stay right where it is."

The lesson here is that we all have the ability to make ourselves more accommodating to others without compromising our ethics, morals and standards or letting anyone walk all over us. When we do this, we can often defuse tensions before they can build into a conflict.

Addressing the problem

Once you've got your own behaviour sorted out, you can look at influencing the actions of others. Mark McGuinness, a business coach from the U.K., offers these four steps for addressing the difficult behaviour of others in his blog, *Wishful Thinking*.

1. Take the "difficult" label off the person. Tell yourself you're dealing with a difficult situation, not a difficult person.
2. Ask yourself, "What do I want them to do?" Be specific in determining your request and remember you're not trying to rebuild their personality, just to influence their behaviour.
3. Next, ask yourself, "What's in it for them to do what I want?" If you can give them a good reason — from their point of view — most likely they will do it.
4. Be firm but friendly. Draw a line through incidents that have happened in the past and focus on the future. Ask for a specific change in behaviour. Point out what they have to gain from changing, and what they have to lose by carrying on as they are.

The four "C's" that will help you get along with almost anybody

Communication

Communication isn't about getting your point across; it is about making a connection with another person. You can do this if you listen more effectively. Contrary to what many people think, communication doesn't begin with talking. Listening is the number one tool in communication, especially when dealing with difficult people. Therefore, seek first to understand by taking the time to listen, reflect and repeat what you are hearing, before you attempt to make your side of the issue understood.

Choose your battles. Chances are, if you have identified an individual as difficult, everything they do will drive you nuts. You need to learn when to speak up and when to walk away. Therefore, choose to focus only on the behaviours at the core of the problem and ignore the rest — both for the sake of your own sanity and to keep the focus on what is important.

If you plan to speak with someone about their behaviour, do it in private. Often when people behave inappropriately, it is because they already have issues with self-esteem. Adding to this by publicly pointing out their faults is counterproductive. Be sure to share your concerns in a respectful way. This is not the time for sarcasm, ridicule or name-calling. Think about how you would want to be treated.

One way to improve communication is to offer training programs for all staff in areas such as negotiation, conflict resolution and active listening. Don't forget to reinforce changes in behaviour with positive comments, even if it is a small change. Everyone likes to know that their efforts are being noticed.

Cooperation
Pointing fingers increases defensiveness and self-justification. It is much more useful to take a cooperative approach

in the way you deal with the situation. Focus on the problem rather than the person and ask for their input in making the situation more workable for both parties. People are much more inclined to follow through with a plan of action when the solution was "their idea" to begin with. Therefore, look for common ground and be predictable in your behaviour. To diminish tensions, be as clear as possible in your dealings with uncooperative counterparts. Announce your intentions and stick to them.

Collaboration

How often do you accomplish a goal or complete a project with no help from others? Likewise, how many of your best ideas have not been made better as a result of input, suggestions or assistance from your colleagues or staff? Engaging the participation of others and subsequently taking the time to thank, reward, recognize and specify the contributions they have made to help you succeed is an essential element of effective work relationships.

Compromise

Many people will reject a compromise simply because they fear that it means they will lose respect or control. In working towards finding a solution to difficult behaviours, try to understand their logic and perspective, and do not underestimate their need for recognition, identity or security. Be willing to acknowledge and address their needs in exchange for a change in behaviour.

It is very interesting to be behind the scenes, but it is not the best place for seeing the play. Try to look out for the good in people and in life and you will see what you look for.
— Sir John Lubbock

TACTICAL MANOEUVRES

- *Keep difficult people in perspective and do not expect them to change. Try to control yourself if you find your feelings getting too intense. Remember that you have options, such as asking for politeness or leaving.*

- *Understand that it's okay to disagree. The important thing is to respect each other's differences so you can maintain a working relationship.*

- *Be patient with yourself. Look at each exchange, whether good or bad, as a lesson on how to deal with others.*

- *You can often turn a bad situation to your advantage by disarming people with kindness and allowing them to feel important.*

- *If possible, plan ahead and prepare your tactics when dealing with a difficult situation. Think about the result you want. Stay calm and keep your emotions under control. Be straightforward and matter-of-fact.*

- *As the guidebook,* Dealing with Difficult People for Dummies, *points out, "gossip and rumours tend to thrive in organizations that don't communicate information well internally. In an information vacuum, people create rumours and gossip to fill the void." If you see a good deal of this type of destructive behaviour in your work environment, make an effort to open up the lines of communication. When real information is available, there is less need to create false information.*

- *Handling personal attacks: Almost every day of your life, someone will say something to you or behave in a way that's clearly designed to offend or annoy. How should you react? The smart answer is: not at all. Most comments and behaviour of this type have one goal in mind, to get a reaction. Letting these small annoyances get to you simply makes you feel bad and gives power to the other person. Unless the situation escalates and the comments turn into harassment, choose to walk away and carry on with your day.*

CHAPTER NINE

Rules of Engagement

Using Etiquette to Ease Awkward Situations

Business is a matter of sentiment and feeling far more than many suppose; everyone likes being treated with kindness and courtesy and a frank, pleasant manner will often clench a bargain more effectively than a half per cent.

I t is often most challenging to be tactful when we are in a new situation where we don't know the rules of etiquette. That is exactly the predicament I found myself in early in my career as a publisher. The occasion was the impending marriage of Princess Diana to Prince Charles, and my wife Kay and I travelled to England because we were doing a special feature for our *TV Week* publication.

I had been granted an interview with the Queen's press secretary in Buckingham Palace at 2 p.m. the day after our arrival.

On the appointed day, I spent the whole morning preparing for the interview, cleaning my shoes, getting my suit ready and making sure that I was presentable. We were staying at the Dorchester Hotel and when it was time to go, we flagged down a cab and once inside, I told the driver, "Buckingham Palace, please."

In making arrangements for the interview, I had received instructions to check in with two police officers in the inner courtyard. So when we arrived at the outside gate that receives all guests, I told the cabbie, "Through the gates, please."

"Not bloody likely," the driver told me.

Just then, a page, who must have been awaiting our arrival, came up and greeted us.

"You're Mr. and Mrs. Legge," he said. "Come with me."

He led us into the palace foyer and put us in a tiny waiting room with very ornate furniture.

As we sat there, the only thing that I could hear in the entire palace was the ticking of the clock in the waiting room. Then, just as the clock struck two, the page returned and said, "Could you follow me, please."

As he led us through the palace, he was going so fast, I could hardly keep up with him as I marvelled at the magnificent decor that surrounded me. There were paintings and busts of previous kings and queens — a 20-foot wide corridor was lined with busts on either side, and I glimpsed a painting of the Coronation of Edward VIII, the biggest painting I'd ever seen in my life.

When we arrived at the press secretary's room, he wasn't there. The page offered us a seat and quickly left. As we looked around at the room, I noticed that there was another door within his office that led directly to the Queen's office. It was somewhat overwhelming to think that at that very moment, I could be sitting mere feet from the Queen herself.

In a minute or two, the press secretary arrived and the interview began. We were there to ask him questions about the wedding of Prince Charles and Princess Diana, which was being put on by the Queen. As we proceeded, the press secretary was very polite, but mostly his answers were limited to yes or no responses, and after seven or eight minutes, he had answered all of the questions I had prepared for him.

I was somewhat perplexed, as I had not yet used up all of my allotted time and yet I had no way to keep the interview going. Foolishly, I said to him, "These paintings are absolutely fabulous. Are they originals?"

He looked at me very steadily and replied, "Mr. Legge, everything in this palace is original."

Not stopping there, I blurted out, "You must have the most interesting public relations job in the world — how do you get a job like that?"

"You don't apply for it," he responded, and the interview was quickly over.

As he escorted us out of the palace, the press secretary was both gracious and kind. As we walked along, he showed us the paintings and the busts and the inner courtyard.

Looking back, I realize that what the press secretary

had in spades was tact. Despite the fact that I had obviously made one or two small faux pas during our interview, rather than become haughty and dismissive, he treated me with respect. No doubt he realized that this was a very exciting moment for me and perhaps even a once-in-a-lifetime experience.

Knowing the rules of etiquette for different situations is very helpful. Most behaviour that is perceived to be disrespectful, discourteous or abrasive is unintentional and could have been avoided by practicing good manners or etiquette. Basic knowledge and practice of etiquette is a valuable tool due to the fact that in many situations a second chance is just not possible or practical.

If you're not sure about a particular setting, do your homework (there are many good books and websites dedicated to the topic) or ask someone who does know. As a public speaker, I've often learned the hard way by sticking my foot in my mouth. One such incident occurred when I was in California some years ago. I was at a Sovereign Order of Saint John of Jerusalem meeting in San Francisco and they asked me to do a toast to the president of the United States — who at that time was Bill Clinton — during the dinner. It was a fabulous black-tie affair with medals and uniforms and all the formality of such events. So I stood up to present the toast and it went something like this:

"Ladies and gentlemen, would you please be upstanding as we toast Bill Clinton, President of the United States."

Given the fact that half of the people in the room were Republicans and the other half Democrats, I was taken aback when a good number of my fellows booed my toast.

As I sat back down, feeling a bit puzzled at the response, one of my American colleagues leaned over and said, "If you're wondering why you got boos, you always toast the office of the President of the United States, never the man. That way, you embrace everybody."

That makes a ton of sense to me and it really illustrates the importance of knowing where you are and whom you're talking to before you open your mouth.

Here's a story about another political toast that went much more smoothly than my own:

Admiral Heihachiro Togo, whose brilliant tactics had destroyed the Russian fleet at the battle of the Sea of Japan in 1905, visited the U.S. shortly after the Russo-Japanese War. At a state dinner in Admiral Togo's honour, William Jennings Bryan was asked to propose a toast. Because Bryan was well known as a strict teetotaler, it was feared that an embarrassing breakdown of protocol was about to occur. But as Bryan stood to propose his toast, he held up his glass and said, "Admiral Togo has won a great victory on water, and I will therefore toast him with water. When Admiral Togo wins a victory on champagne, I will toast him with champagne."

I admire the tactful way in which Mr. Bryan was able to honour his own convictions as someone who did not partake of alcohol while still rising to the occasion of the toast. His ability to do so shows a high regard for the feelings of others, in addition to whatever moral convictions he might hold for himself. When it comes to deeply held beliefs, it is often difficult for us to hold those who do not share our beliefs in the same high regard as we hold those who do. This lack of respect is often what leads us to act in a tactless manner.

When it comes to etiquette, courtesy and consideration go hand in hand with tact. Being courteous includes polite behaviour (the manners your mother taught you) and the willingness and generosity to extend assistance when it is needed. This includes gestures such as holding the door open for others, tidying up the room after a meeting even if it isn't "in your job description," or giving up your seat on the bus to someone who is elderly, pregnant or infirm.

The late Colonel Bill McKinney of the Royal Westminster Regiment in New Westminster, British Columbia, shortly before his death, asked me if I would be willing to serve my country for a three-year period as an honorary lieutenant colonel of that proud and distinguished regiment.

Of course I said yes, in part because Colonel McKinney wasn't one to take no for an answer, but mostly because I was honoured to be asked and because my father, who was a tireless volunteer for a number of civic endeavours in the Royal City, would have been thrilled to know that I was contributing to the community he loved so much.

Unfortunately, I never had the privilege of serving under Colonel McKinney — who proudly served the regiment for some 50 years and received many medal recognitions, including the Order of British Columbia — however, I did serve under the equally dedicated Colonel Les Deane, CM, who has written a book titled *The Officers' Mess*, a guide to the rules governing dress, etiquette and customs for the officers' mess.

Although the book is meant specifically for military personnel, in reading through it, I couldn't help but be reminded of a time gone by when good manners, rules of etiquette and a general sense of regard for one's fellows were attributes that most of us held in high esteem.

"A well-mannered mess is one where proper respect is shown to senior officers, and sincere friendliness to equals and subordinates," wrote Colonel Deane. "There may be certain officers whom you find difficult to understand, or like; do not let this in any way impair your good manners."

He also advised, "To wear improper dress or sloppy clothing advertises the fact that the person so doing is lacking in ordinary good manners. Courtesy requires that you dress in accordance with the accepted custom. Officers should always wear the dress appropriate to the occasion."

And, "Good manners require you to make visitors to your mess feel at home. If they are unaccompanied, rise to meet them when they enter the mess, and try to entertain them until the particular officer they are visiting arrives. If you invite a guest to the mess, you should be there to greet him when he arrives."

In addition, Colonel Deane's book offers an A to Z listing of tips for junior officers. These tips offer common-sense advice that can easily be applied to any social or business situation.

"If you receive a formal invitation to attend any mess function, in your own, or another mess, you must reply in writing, either accepting or declining the invitation in the prescribed manner. Failure to reply to an invitation shows bad manners and a lack of consideration." [With so many functions to attend, it is easy to let this one slip. Make a point to answer invitations as soon as possible after you receive them, even if you cannot attend. It's a sure way to keep your name on the guest list for next time.]

"An officer must not only be punctual for parades but for meetings and social functions as well. If an officer is wise, he will arrive five minutes ahead of time so as not to have the embarrassment of having to apologize for being late." [Being punctual is one of the best ways to show others that you respect their time.]

"If speeches are made after dinner, give the speaker a courteous hearing, even if he fails to be witty, or is inaudible to you." [i.e., This is not the time to check the email on your BlackBerry or play a game on your cell phone.]

Good advice for the military and good advice for all of us civilians.

Extending courtesy is about making the effort to be nice and although it often requires nothing more than a small gesture on your part, it often results in immediate rewards. These include: other people reciprocating with nice gestures of their own; an increase in your popularity (people want to be around you because you're friendly and pleasant); and a positive shift in the overall tone of your interactions with others.

As with courtesy, consideration involves thoughtful concern for the welfare of others and respect for the needs, feelings, opinions and rights of others even if they are not in alignment with our own. It also requires the ability to put our own desires on the backburner when the situation calls for us to do so.

Consideration is the act of giving what is needed without expecting anything in return. In the workplace, being considerate could involve helping a new person get their bearings, pitching in to allow someone to honour family commitments, or offering to pick up a hot meal for a colleague who's working overtime to meet a tight deadline. Often, these are the small touches that people will remember for years to come.

It's human nature to want to be liked. In most situations in life, you will be able to accomplish more if people like you. After all, people would rather do business with someone they like. An easy way to build rapport with almost anyone is to take the time to notice something about them.

Think about the last time someone paid you a compliment you felt was genuine or struck up a conversation about something that you were doing, reading or making. Didn't it make you feel good about yourself and that person? Pay attention to someone and often their affection and respect for you will increase significantly, and it doesn't matter who they are — from the CEO of a top company to the doorman or security guard at your office building, to the child of a colleague or acquaintance you meet on the street — everyone likes to be acknowledged.

Another way to build rapport is to offer your assistance in a time of need. That's how I came to know one of Vancouver's most endearing personalities. Here's what happened.

If you've read any of my previous books, you will already know that I have always believed that it is almost impossible for anyone to succeed in his or her chosen profession without the help of many others — and when I returned to Canada in 1969 after an 18-month tour in the entertainment business, I knew that I needed help to re-establish myself with some local gigs.

Thankfully, my Vancouver agent, showman Ben Kopelow, had booked me into Ken Stauffer's Cave Supper Club on Hornby Street as the opening act for the world-famous Mills Brothers. Back in those days, The Cave was a very big deal both in Vancouver and internationally; so too were the Mills Brothers.

Unfortunately, I was not really prepared from a sartorial point of view for my big debut back in Vancouver (i.e., I had no money to buy a proper suit to wear). The fact of the matter was that while I had been successful from an artistic point of view during the 18 months I had spent in England — doing television shows, radio, dozens of nightclub engagements, appearances at U.S. military bases and even a gig at the famous Playboy Club in Pall Mall — I came back to Vancouver literally flat broke.

So there I was, set to open at The Cave in seven days, doing two shows a night for two weeks and I had nothing to wear.

Enter character Murray Goldman, one of Canada's premier clothiers, a man who through unique advertising had earned himself a larger-than-life status (outside of business, he used his considerable promotional skills to help Big Brothers, a cause to which he was devoted).

Murray came to the rescue. He invited me to his Hastings Street headquarters and told me to pick out five or six outfits: suits, ties, shirts, whatever I needed. He would have them tailored and ready by opening night.

"Pay me when you can, Peter," he said. "You *have* to look good at The Cave. And I'll be there opening night to make sure you do."

I walked onto the stage on opening night looking great

and feeling confident, thanks to Murray and his generosity. Thankfully, several more Cave assignments followed and it wasn't long before I was back on my feet.

Although The Cave is long gone today and I moved from comedy to publishing and public speaking, I will never forget how Murray helped me. He truly is one of those people who are ready when we need them to help us along. Murray didn't ask questions or look for IOUs, he came right out with a tape measure and went to work.

And of course, he was there on opening night with his smile as big as ever.

Murray did it in his special way and because of that, when, from time to time I've seen an opportunity to help someone else, I have followed his lead and jumped in to help.

This story remained a relative secret for many years until the Big Brothers of Vancouver held a roast to honour Murray for his many decades of unselfish support. They asked me to be one of the speakers at the roast where I told this story to the more than 1,000 gathered guests. It was one more way of reimbursing Murray Goldman for the generous contribution he made to my show business career.

*He had occasional flashes of silence that made
his conversation perfectly delightful.*
— Sydney Smith

What of the etiquette of others?
If and when you feel it necessary to correct the behaviour

of others, it is important to keep your focus on the positive. For example, perhaps you have a young person in your organization whose choice of clothing is either too "edgy," too casual or too revealing for the image of your company.

Rather than chastising this individual for making poor choices, you could broach the subject by saying something like this: "You've got a great future here and I'd like to see you make the most of your opportunity for advancement. Here are some guidelines that will help you understand the manner of attire that is desirable here." Given this approach, I think most people interested in advancement would take the recommendations to heart and rethink their business wardrobe.

> *Conversation is an art in itself and it is by no means those who have the most to tell who are the best talkers.*
>
> — Sir John Lubbock

TACTICAL MANOEUVRES

- *Contrary to what some people might think, being in a position of power, whether it is within a business, family, community group or any other organization, does not give any person the right to berate, belittle, intimidate or ridicule another human being. As your mother taught you, if you can't say anything nice — or say it in a tactful way — don't say anything at all. The same goes for bullies whom you might encounter; don't be afraid to respectfully remind them that personal attacks are unacceptable. If that doesn't work, it is best to refrain from doing business with them in the future.*

- *While serving clients or customers, pay them the compliment of your undivided attention. Few things are as annoying as waiting for service while the person assisting you stops to chat with a colleague or answer the phone to help someone else. If you must answer the phone, take the number and tell the caller you'll phone them back. The customer who is in front of you should always be your priority.*

- *Always return calls. Even if you don't yet have an answer to the caller's question, call and explain what you're doing to fulfill their request, or direct them to the appropriate place to get what they need.*

- *Make sure your voicemail system is working properly and doesn't tell the caller that the mailbox is full, transfer them to nowhere or ring indefinitely. Address technical and system problems — a dysfunctional machine or system is as unacceptable as a rude person.*

- *Personalize your electronic interactions. Many people behave in electronic media (including phone, voicemail and email) the same way that they behave when driving their car in rush-hour traffic. They feel that since they're not face-to-face with a person, it is perfectly acceptable to be abrupt, tactless or rude. Your electron-*

ic communications deserve the same level of formality as your personal interactions.

- *Before you attend an event, use your electronic database or address book to refresh your memory about the people who are likely to be attending as well. People are always impressed when you can remember their name and can recall something specific about them.*

- *Always pass along credit and compliments to everyone who made a contribution to a successful undertaking. Speak well of your co-workers and when appropriate, point out their accomplishments to others. Appearing to have taken the credit to impress a boss or customer is the surest way to sabotage a relationship with a co-worker.*

- *When mingling or networking with others, never talk for more than a minute without pausing and giving others a chance to join in. The entire purpose of social gatherings is to make connections and you can hardly do that if you are not open to learning more about the interests and ideas of others.*

- *Always apologize if you must interrupt a conversation, meeting or someone's concentration on a task. Quickly state the nature of what you need, and show consideration for the fact that you are interrupting valuable work or progress.*

- *Take the time to show that you are thoughtful by acknowledging special occasions. Send cards or letters for birthdays or congratulations of promotions or other events, send flowers for engagements, weddings or in condolence for the death of someone's loved one or family member. People will often remember your kindness much longer than you can imagine.*

- *Make your goodbyes memorable. The Four Seasons Hotel in Seattle makes departure from the hotel as memorable as the stay. Visitors leaving the hotel and travelling by car are sent on their way with a little white box filled with cookies and a container of cold milk to make the trip more enjoyable. Look for ways that you can leave a lasting impression on your own customers.*

CHAPTER TEN

The Power of Apology

Taking Your Foot Out of Your Mouth When You've Said or Done Something You Regret

Never ruin an apology with an excuse.

An authentic apology relays a genuine concern for the other person's feelings and well-being and is based on empathy for the injured party. A thoughtful apology can mend a relationship by melting away hurt, anger and resentment and allow you to begin to reconnect with the other person. A thoughtless one, on the other hand, may have the opposite effect, causing more injury and further conflict.

What makes an effective apology?

Many mediation and reconciliation experts agree that there are four basic steps to an effective apology:

1. Admit that you have done something wrong and are willing to make it right.

2. Acknowledge the damage done to the other person as a result of your actions.

3. Ask for forgiveness (this is a very humbling experience and much more powerful than simply saying, "I'm sorry"). Asking someone to forgive you acknowledges that damage has been done to the relationship and that some healing needs to take place. It can also begin to bridge the gap that the damage has caused.

4. Ask the person you have hurt what you can do to repair the relationship.

> *What makes an apology work is the exchange of shame and power between the offender and the offended.*
> — Aaron Lazare

Rosamund Stone Zander, who is a psychotherapist and the co-author of *The Art of Possibility*, takes a different approach that I think can be equally effective for people who find it difficult to apologize in the manner stated above.

"I realized that there were two kinds of apologies," Zander explained in her essay, *The Power of an Apology*, published in the July 2001 edition of *Parade Magazine.* "In one, someone admits she is wrong, the other person gets his revenge, and justice is served. The second type is as different as love to war. In this one, a person notices that something is broken and finds a way to make it whole again."

Zander goes on to explain that we get so caught up in figuring out who is right and who is wrong that we forget what matters.

"Once you realize you don't have to make yourself wrong to deliver an apology, you'll feel a new power. If you differ strongly with a friend on a political matter, you can say: 'My passion for my own beliefs has made it difficult for me to fully understand yours. If it has caused trouble between us, I apologize. My relationship with you is far more important than whether we agree or not.' And if you have a strained situation with your boss and feel misunderstood, at least you can say, 'I'm sorry for the tension that has developed between us. I intend to find a way to work it out.' We cannot always act in perfect harmony with the people around us. They inevitably will feel upset, misunderstood and frustrated by things we do. But we don't have to get so caught up with figuring out who is right and who is wrong that we forget what matters. The power of an apology does not lie in the admission of guilt. An apology is a tool to re-establish our connection with others when something has damaged it."

Zander encourages us to think of any breakdown between us and another person as an opportunity to apologize. A breakdown is evident anytime you feel angry, tense, disapproving, distant, sad or vengeful toward someone.

As Zander and many other experts have observed, people often shy away from apologizing out of fear of humiliation, showing weakness, loss of power, respect or control, or of being sued by the offended party.

If you are someone who resists apologizing when you know that you should, ask yourself this question, "Who do you respect more: someone who can never admit to a mistake, or someone who acknowledges their shortcomings and tries to make amends for them?"

Don't apologize unless you mean it

If an apology does not feel sincere, it can further damage the relationship. Sincerity is expressed by what you say, how you say it, and what body language you use. An inadequate or insincere apology can feel dismissive to the offended party and may heighten conflict.

Apology is an important part of taking responsibility for our actions. Apology opens a door, allowing us an opportunity to do better next time, and it sets a positive example for those around us.

"Failure to admit error and express regret adds insult to injury and is one of the most blatant ways of showing disrespect," revealed Beverly Engel in her book, *The Power of Apology*.

This is as true for organizations and businesses as it is for individuals.

On the other side of the coin, imagine how you would feel as a customer, if you were the recipient of a letter like this one, sent by JetBlue, a U.S.-based airline company, following a particularly bad week.

Dear JetBlue Customers,
We are sorry and embarrassed. But most of all, we are deeply sorry.
Last week was the worst operational week in JetBlue's seven-year history. Following the severe winter ice storm in the Northeast, we subjected our customers to unacceptable delays, flight cancellations, lost baggage and other major inconveniences. The storm disrupted the movement of aircraft, and, more importantly, disrupted the movement of JetBlue's pilot and inflight crew members who were depending on those planes to get them to the airports where they were scheduled to serve you. With the busy President's Day weekend upon us, rebooking opportunities were scarce and hold times at 1-800-JETBLUE were unacceptably long or not even available, further hindering our recovery efforts.
Words cannot express how truly sorry we are for the anxiety, frustration and inconvenience that we caused. This is especially saddening because JetBlue was founded on the promise of bringing humanity back to air travel and making the experience of flying happier and easier for everyone who chooses to fly with us. We know we

failed to deliver on this promise last week.

We are committed to you, our valued customers, and are taking immediate corrective steps to regain your confidence in us. We have begun putting a comprehensive plan in place to provide better and more timely information to you, more tools and resources for our crewmembers and improved procedures for handling operational difficulties in the future. We are confident, as a result of these actions, that JetBlue will emerge as a more reliable and even more customer responsive airline than ever before.

Most importantly, we have published the JetBlue Airways Customer Bill of Rights — our official commitment to you of how we will handle operational interruptions going forward — including details of compensation. I have a video message to share with you about this industry-leading action.

You deserved better — a lot better — from us last week. Nothing is more important than regaining your trust and all of us here hope you will give us the opportunity to welcome you onboard again soon and provide you the positive JetBlue Experience you have come to expect from us.

Sincerely,
David Neeleman
Founder and CEO
JetBlue Airways

To err is human, but when the eraser wears out ahead of the pencil, you're overdoing it.
— Josh Jenkins

TACTICAL MANOEUVRES

- *You can't excuse your way to success. When you've made a mistake, it's not enough to make yourself feel better; the important thing is to make the individual or organization you have injured feel better and then correct the problem to ensure that it doesn't happen again.*

- *It is important to accept responsibility for your actions. You don't have to admit to the whole world that you made a mistake, but you do have to admit it to yourself and anyone else who will be affected by it — and the sooner the better.*

- *Never use your authority to mask a mistake. If you make one, admit it, explain it, apologize for it and above all else, learn from it. Allowing others to see that you accept responsibility and learn from your errors can go a long way towards healing any loss of faith.*

- *Apology is important to our emotional and physical well-being and for many of us, the inability to apologize can become the source of a great deal of dysfunction and unhappiness in all aspects of our lives.*

- *If you do make an error, admit it and apologize imme-*

diately. People tend to be very responsive to an appeal for forgiveness in the face of an honest mistake. Ninety-five per cent of customers will do business with you again if you resolve the problem immediately.

- *Admit your mistakes, but don't overanalyze them. Despite the fact that you messed up, there is no need to wallow in endless rounds of shoulda, coulda, woulda. Once you've corrected your error, look to the future.*

- *Don't be afraid to laugh at your mistakes. The ability to see humour in a problem can make the lesson it has to teach us much more palatable. Former NBA centre and coach Johnny Kerr tells a story about coaching the Chicago Bulls back in the 1960s. At the time, Kerr was struggling with the challenges of coaching an expansion team and in the midst of a major losing streak, he tried to pump up the team by giving them a pre-game pep talk before they headed out onto the floor in Boston. During the talk, Kerr told Bob Boozer to pretend he was the best scorer in basketball, he told Jerry Sloan to pretend he could stop anyone in the game, then he told Guy Rodgers to pretend he was the top point guard in the league, and finally, he told six-foot-eight Erwin Mueller to pretend he was a shot-blocking rebounding machine.*

"We played the Celtics at the Garden and lost by 17 points," Kerr recalls. "So I was pacing around the locker room afterward, trying to figure out what to say to the team when Mueller walked up, put his arm around me and said, 'Don't worry about it, coach. Just pretend we won.'"

- *In Vancouver, there is a local company called Acme Humble Pie that has taken the art of the apology to a whole new level. They can deliver a "humble pie" anywhere in Canada and each pie is packaged in its own crate with a personalized note. My company, Canada Wide Media Limited, has used them a few times (thankfully, we don't qualify for the frequent-flyer discount) and everyone we have sent them to has been extremely touched by the gesture. If you need to apologize, try some humble pie — it sure beats eating crow.*

CONCLUSION

Use your head. Consult your reason. It is not infallible, but you will be less likely to err if you do so.

This past spring, my wife Kay and I went on a Mediterranean cruise that included stops in Italy. While there, we signed up for a day trip to see the city of Florence. Disembarking from the ship in the morning, there were about 30 of us travelling together on a coach. The excursion was to be 10 hours in total, including a two-hour bus ride to Florence followed by a walking tour around the city, lunch and a return trip of two hours.

As we prepared to leave, our tour guide, Ricardo Nesti — who has some 30 years of experience on the job — stepped onto the bus and gave us an outline of the tour in addition to mentioning the fact that there were no toilets on the coach and very few facilities at the places we would be visiting throughout the day. Therefore, to ensure that no one would be caught in an embarrassing situation, our guide very tactfully came up with a plan to manage bathroom breaks.

"Because we have so many nationalities, I'm not going to refer to it as the loo or the toilet or what have you," he informed us. "Instead, I'm going to refer to it as 'the situation.' I don't want to be on the bus halfway to Florence and find out that someone here hasn't taken care of the situation."

Considering the variety of languages spoken among the group and the mix of ladies and gentlemen of a certain age, this was far better — and more tactful — in my mind, than continually asking a bunch of adults if they had remembered to go to the washroom.

As it turned out, we were happy with our guide's foresight in dealing with bathroom breaks; Florence is a beautiful city with much to see and we did a great deal of walking that day — something that would be far less enjoyable had we been constantly concerned with finding a bathroom.

Our guide wasn't exaggerating either about the scarcity of facilities. When we stopped for lunch at Ristorante Paoli, which was housed in a beautiful 13th-century building, there was only one washroom in this old building and therefore we had to orchestrate the timing of our visits so that everyone could "take care of the situation" before it was time to climb back on the coach.

Some had to go after the first drink, some after the salad, some after the main course and so on. With careful planning and scheduling, we all managed to take care of the situation and as a result, the phrase became a bit of an inside joke with our little group of travellers as we turned to ask each other the question each time we got back on the bus after visiting a point of interest.

Later that day as we prepared to get back on the bus for the return trip, our guide tactfully reminded us with his by-then signature phrase.

"I don't want the situation to get out of control on our two-hour bus ride back," he warned. "Have you taken care of the situation?"

One by one as we stepped onto the coach, we smiled, nodded and assured him that we had, indeed, taken care of the situation.

As the bus pulled up to the ship and we prepared to bid farewell to our guide, one of the passengers piped up and said, "This brings a whole new meaning to the musical *Oliver Twist* and the song that was sung by Fagan, 'I'm reviewing the situation.'"

One side note about Florence; it is one of those cities with so much history that you could spend a whole year exploring and still not be able to see it all. The first museum we visited in Florence is the one that houses Michelangelo's statue of David, which was truly awe inspiring. Our next stop was a cathedral that holds the tombs of many famous people, including Galileo, and opposite from there was the place where Michelangelo is buried. We were eager to drink it all in and our tour guide was excellent. In fact, I told my wife, if he had been a professor at university when I was studying history, I definitely would have gotten an "A." If you've never been to Florence, I would definitely recommend it.

So what is Tact, really?

Is it, in fact, an out-of-date concept, or is it in reality one of the most important and enduring universal principles? For me, it is as simple as doing unto others as you would want them to do unto you. I have always believed that in business and community life, you will never err if you always choose to go about your business with generosity, grace and diplomacy as your guiding principles. Like so many of the important things in life, tact is simple, but not always easy. It requires effort and a willingness to put others first.

How can putting others first help us to be successful in our own lives?

Let me take you back to a meeting I attended at the world headquarters of The Salvation Army on Peter's Hill in London, England. In a simple office on the third floor was the home of the 18th general of The Salvation Army, Clifton Shaw. As basic as the room was, however, it had a very special feature, a floor-to-ceiling window with a direct and unobstructed view of Christopher Wren's edifice, St. Paul's Cathedral — a magnificent cathedral that by some miraculous intervention was spared from bombing in the Second World War. With its splendid dome, soaring arches and intricate carving, I expect that a constant view of this masterpiece could inspire one on a daily basis. Even more inspiring is the fact that for an entire century after Wren's death, St Paul's remained a unique achievement in the world: the only cathedral to have been built by a single architect and completed within his lifetime (building commenced in 1675 and the final stone was laid on the Lantern in October 1708, on Sir Christopher's 76th birthday).

So there I was in Clifton Shaw's office, admiring the view when I noticed off in one corner sitting on the floor was a magnificent bust of William Booth, the founder of The Salvation Army and the army's first general (whom I mentioned earlier in this volume). As I walked over to take a closer look at this bust, I asked (the current general) my host Bill Francis, now the commissioner for Canada, if there were one memorable story about William Booth that exemplified what we could learn from his example. In response to my question, he relayed the story of how, as The Salvation Army's general, Booth had once been asked to telegraph his offices and use just one word to describe what The Salvation Army was all about. After much thought, the one simple word he came up with was OTHERS.

"It's not about us," he said, "it's about OTHERS."

As I mentioned in Chapter 8, according to a study done by Booz Allen Hamilton, The Salvation Army is one of the 10 most successful organizations in the world, and William Booth's philosophy — that it's always about others — has stood the test of time.

Tact, too, is about considering the needs of others and I believe it may just be one of the most overlooked success secrets in the world.

Imagine the impact each one of us could have if we changed this one simple aspect of our thinking . . .

It's not about us, it's about our spouse,
it's not about us, it's about our children,
it's not about us, it's about our friends,
it's not about us, it's about our colleagues,
it's not about us, it's about our neighbours,
it's not about us, it's about our customers,
it's not about us, it's about our community,
it's not about us, it's about others.

Fellow public speaker Zig Ziglar once said, "You can have everything you want in life if you help enough other people get what they want in life." The success we experience in life is in direct proportion to another universal principle, that of sowing and reaping:

If you sow nothing (by being selfish and only doing that which benefits you directly), you will reap nothing.

If you sow plenty (by investing in others and helping them to get what they want), you will reap plenty.

Likewise, as the prophets say, "If you sow to the wind [being careless with your words and actions], you will reap a whirlwind [chaos and destruction]."

People respond to how you treat them and how you make them feel. If you treat them with respect, empathy, thoughtfulness, consideration and acceptance, most people will rise to the occasion and do everything in their power to live up to your expectations and reciprocate in kind.

The opportunity to spread the word about "OTHERS"

Knowing that I am a voracious reader, a little more than a year ago, my friend Tom Skidmore sent me a copy of the book, *The Salvation Army*, by Robert A. Watson, to read. I was so impressed with the book that I asked Tom for more copies, only to find that none were available.

Not ready to give up on finding more copies, I tracked down the publisher, Random House in New York, and was told the book was out of print. So I took the next step and contacted the author, Robert Watson, to find out who owned the intellectual property rights to the book. Commissioner Watson informed me the rights were held by Random House.

Wanting to help me get access to more copies of the book, Commissioner Watson agreed to assist in the process of getting the rights returned to The Salvation Army and himself (as author). After much negotiation and discussion, I paid Random House to return the rights to The Salvation Army and Commissioner Watson, and upon discovering that I was a publisher, they offered me the book's publishing rights for Canada.

Of course, I jumped at the opportunity to publish the book and have it distributed across the country. To date, more than 30,000 books, with a value of $600,000, have been given away to municipal, provincial and federal officials, in addition to thousands of supporters of The Salvation Army.

Why did I do this? Simply put, I did it because The Salvation Army exemplifies in an organization the character traits that we need to have as individuals. As a result, they have probably done more to relieve suffering and offer redemption and hope (to those who need it the most) than any other organization in the history of the world. That's an accomplishment to be proud of.

George Bernard Shaw once said, "Without good manners, human society becomes intolerable and impossible."

And Blaise Pascal said, "Kind words do not cost much, yet they accomplish much."

People do business with people they like

Another port of call on our Seabourn cruise in the Mediterranean this past spring was St. Tropez. La Citadelle is a landmark walled fortress atop St. Tropez's central hill. The fortress has guarded this famed city in the south of France for four centuries and according to legend, a Roman soldier gave the town its name. Today, St. Tropez is a fairy-tale port city best known as a playground for billionaires and their gigantic yachts, which fill up the picturesque harbour.

Dozens of painters selling "their" original works lined the Quai H. Bouchard as my wife and I were whisked by on a two-hour walking tour of the city.

The French artist Henri Matisse once said, "There is nothing more difficult for a truly creative painter than to paint a rose because before he can do so, he must first forget all the roses that were ever painted."

Much the same can be said of painting a famous spot like St. Tropez.

Following the tour, I knew that a painting of the harbour had to be bought and taken home for my collection. Therefore, after visiting the cathedral, the Place des Lices market (which is only open Tuesday and Saturday mornings) and the beach where Brigitte Bardot filmed Roger Vadim's *And God Created Woman*, we perused the vendors on the Quai and found just the right piece to buy.

The woman who served us told me that her husband painted the canvases and she sold them. After we picked out our painting, I asked her, "Do you take Visa?"

"Of course," she replied. "But I have no electricity here."

So she left her stand with about 50 paintings on easels, with no security, and walked us over to a bureau de change and facilitated our getting 200 Euros in cash. I was impressed that instead of just pointing us in the direction, she took the time and the risk of leaving her kiosk unattended to walk with us and make sure we were looked after.

At that moment, it didn't matter that we weren't billionaires with a big fancy yacht in the harbour; as a result of her one small gesture, the lady who sold her husband's paintings made us feel as if we were the most important customers in the world. Although we need to remind ourselves of it from time to time, it doesn't take much effort to make a big difference. Applying the Power of Tact to your everyday life can help you reach your goals, your dreams and your aspirations.

In closing, I'd like to say thank you to Sir John Lubbock for writing the book that introduced Tact into my life, and thank you to my father, Bernard Lawrence Legge, for modelling a life of significance that at its central core was all about Tact. To everyone who reads this book, I wish you great success in applying the Power of Tact to your own life.

Best wishes,

Peter Legge
Vancouver, 2008

About the Author

Dr. Peter Legge, L.L.D. (HON) • CSP • CPAE • HOF

Peter Legge is President and CEO of Canada Wide Media Limited, the largest independently owned publishing company in Western Canada, controlling a network of 47 magazines across the country with over $30 million in sales annually.

In addition, Peter travels the world as a motivational speaker, accepting more than 100 assignments each year from clients who know that when he speaks, his words will be a catalyst for positive change. He has received the prestigious Golden Gavel Award from Toastmasters International and was voted "Top Speaker in North America," in company with Dr. Robert Schuller and Stephen Covey. Peter has also been inducted into the Speakers Hall of Fame by both the National Speakers Association in the United States and the Canadian Association of Professional Speakers.

Peter is tireless in his commitments to many worthwhile organizations. As co-host of the annual Variety — The Children's Charity Telethon for 30 consecutive years, he has assisted in raising more than $130 million for the charity. He is also an International Ambassador for Variety International.

His efforts have not gone unnoticed. Among his many honours, Peter has received the Golden Heart Award from The Variety Club and has been invested into the Venerable Order of St. John of Jerusalem, where he was recently promoted to Commander.

He has been awarded the Order of the Red Cross and named Citizen of the Year for his commitment to the community. Simon Fraser University recently honoured him with an Honorary Doctor of Laws Degree, and he is a past Chair of the Vancouver Board of Trade.

He is the recipient of the Nido Qubein Philanthropy Award presented to him at the NSA Convention in Atlanta in July 2005.

In 2006, he was appointed one of 18 ambassadors to the Vancouver 2010 Olympic and Paralympic Winter Games. In the same year, Sales and Marketing Executives International awarded Peter with the Ambassador of Free Enterprise in Dallas, Texas.

Peter is also the author of 10 previous books that have inspired thousands of readers the world over with their powerful motivating messages. In all that he has achieved, Peter attributes his success to four factors: persistence, patience, a positive attitude and passion.

To contact Peter Legge, write to:

Peter Legge Management Company Ltd.
4180 Lougheed Highway, 4th Floor
Burnaby, BC V5C 6A7 Canada
Telephone: 604-299-7311
Email: plegge@canadawide.com
Website: *www.peterlegge.com*

* To book Peter Legge to speak at your next convention, AGM or association meeting, call Lea Ortner, Podium Presentations, manager of speaker services for Peter Legge. (250) 248-5732 *leaortner@shaw.ca*